WEALTH WORKOUT

WEALTH WORKOUT

H.D. Vest's Wealth Building Program for Life

H.D. Vest, MS, MSFS, MSM, DIBA, CEBS,
CFA, CFP, CFS, ChFC, CLU, CMA,
CPA/PFS, FLMI/M, AMC, EPTC, PECC

Lynn R. Niedermeier, CPA, CFS

IRWIN
Professional Publishing®
Chicago • London • Singapore

Irwin Professional Book Team

Publisher:	Wayne McGuirt
Associate publisher:	Jeffery A. Krames
Executive editor:	Amy Hollands Gaber
Managing editor:	Kevin Thornton
Senior marketing manager:	Tiffany Dykes
Project editor:	Jane Lightell
Production supervisor:	Lara Feinberg
Compositor:	Desktop Miracles
Typeface:	11/13 Palatino
Printer:	Quebecor Book Press

T Times Mirror
M Higher Education Group

Library of Congress Cataloging-in-Publication Data

Vest, Herb D.
    Wealth workout : H. D. Vest's wealth building program for life / Herb D. Vest, Lynn R. Niedermeier.
        p. cm.
    ISBN 0-7863-0467-7
    1. Finance, Personal.   2. Wealth   I. Niedermeier, Lynn.   II. Title.
HG179 IN PROCESS
332.024—dc20   95–38590

Printed in the United States of America
1 2 3 4 5 6 7 8 9 0 Q 2 1 0 9 8 7 6 5

contents

warm-up

EXERCISE
ONE

EXERCISE
TWO

EXERCISE
SIX

Weeks 8 & 9   Reward Yourself   125

Warm-Up Exercise
Rewards Worksheet
Four Investment Strategies
Strategic Asset Allocation
Diversification
Dollar-Cost Averaging
Buy-Hold

EXERCISE
SEVEN

Week 10   Tax Attack   139

Warm-Up Exercise
Tax Attack Worksheet
How To Reduce Your Taxes
Municipal Bonds and Bond Funds
401 (k) Plans
403 (b) Plans
IRA
Annuities
SEP - IRA
SAR - SEP
Keogh

EXERCISE
EIGHT

Week 11   Protecting Your Gluteus Maximus   159

Warm-Up Exercise
Gluteus Maximus Worksheet
Three Major Areas of Insurance
Life Insurance
Disability Insurance
Long-Term Healthcare
Property and Casualty
Major Medical/Health
Elder Care
Estate Planning

EXERCISE
NINE

closing remarks

acknowledgments

We believe that the American public must be served by honest, professional, and highly educated individuals in the area of financial services. It is significant to the financial survival of our families, parents, children, and, we believe, the United States. We must take responsibility for ourselves and educate our children about critical financial issues that will affect them for a lifetime, which could make it or break it for them in having a decent and dignified standard of living.

Thousands of professional men and women also believe this and have become associated with H.D. Vest Financial Services in an effort to make a difference in the lives of the people they care about most—their clients.

We want to thank these individuals for their dedication and commitment to their clients and for being an important part of changing the way America invests.

We also want to thank our families, who have been patient and supportive. Without their love and encouragement this company would not be where it is today and this book would not have been written. Our gratitude to Ruth and Horace Powers, Barbara Vest, Matthew and Daniel Vest, Art and Ruth Niedermeier, and Erica and Beau Niedermeier. We would especially like to thank Michael Vlies for the significant amount of time and effort he contributed to assisting us in developing and completing this book. His contributions were invaluable.

We would also like to thank our associates at H.D. Vest who assisted and contributed their technical expertise: Roger Ochs, JD, MBA, CFP; Carolyn Jergens, CIMC, CFP, CFS; Jeanne Glorioso, CFP; Jeff Klein, CFP, CFS; David O'Neill, CFP; Shannon Soefje, CFS; Maurice Olson; MBA, CFA, CFP, CFS; and Karen Pinion, CFP.

A special thanks goes to Sandra Raesz for her patience in compiling the many drafts we prepared and the superior product that always resulted and to Jan Schmidt for her thoughtful suggestions on ways to improve the readability of the book.

Finally, we thank the thousands of American families and small businesses that have discovered the wisdom of financial planning through H.D. Vest's network of tax and financial professionals. If you are not currently among them, we hope that through this book you soon will be.

warm-up

YOU ARE ABOUT TO ENTER A NEW KIND OF FITNESS PROGRAM

- A one-of-a-kind FINANCIAL WORKOUT that will walk you through simple and painless exercises to achieve your financial goals.
- A workout that takes the ingredients from the gobbledygook financial experts, tosses them into a blender at high speed, and then pours out for you a tasteful concoction that will quench your thirst for straightforward financial information.
- Quite simply, WE BELIEVE that *Wealth Workout* will provide you with all of the tools you could possibly need to personalize your very own wealth-building workout for life!

Who will pay the bills if I'm disabled?

What if I'm laid off?

When will I be able to retire?

Where will the money come from?

How will I survive?

If you are like millions of working Americans who anguish over these questions every waking day of your life, you will be pleased to know that you are holding in your hands a common-sense program of FINANCIAL FITNESS that will extinguish these fears, putting YOU in charge of your financial future!

Your first step before embarking upon this program is to make an honest COMMITMENT to yourself that you will follow our innovative wealth-building program, step-by-step, for 90 days.

Wealth Workout will provide you with the tools and the financial exercises you need to succeed with your personal financial fitness plan. We have included weekly progress charts. If you become bogged down, we offer guidance on how to identify the

> **Lazy hands make a man poor, but diligent hands bring wealth.**
> *Proverbs 10:4*

most appropriate personal money trainer. However, it is imperative that you commit to *full* participation on a daily basis for 90 days. Nothing else will do. If you are unable to make this commitment, our deepest regrets. Go ahead and return this book to the shelf and continue the struggle to understand the gobbledygook.

Wealth Workout will do for your financial life what a powerful weight-reduction program can do for your physical life. Put simply, it provides an easy-to-follow, 12-week program that prepares you for a lifetime of fitness, the type of strong financial fitness that will help you to reach out and touch all of the financial goals of your life, such as a new home for your family, college funding for your children, funding to care for older family members, and a secure and comfortable retirement for yourself.

Whether your goal is to reverse a financial fiasco by bringing discipline into your life or simply to refine your wealth-building approach—adding to the assets you have already accumulated—this book will get you there.

So for the next 90 days, forget *everything* that your uncle, friends, co-workers, and talk show guests have advised or preached to you about building wealth. Clean the slate. Cleanse the mind. All you need is *Wealth Workout*, your strongest commitment, and some good, old-fashioned discipline.

Whatever "wealth" means to you—$100,000, $1 million, or more—you can achieve it by getting your hands on a common-sense program that can make it happen, a program that will balance your current lifestyle with your future needs. Millions of Americans have learned to achieve wealth for generations. However, as our society becomes more complicated, Americans who wish to save for retirement believe that many of the conventional assumptions that go into wealth building no longer apply.

After all, the conventional definition of the *nuclear family*—husband, wife, two children, and a dog—applies to fewer and fewer American households. Singles, for example, aren't always "single"—some have lifetime partners. Other families have two or more different sets of children, with one set old enough to drive the other set to day care. It is no wonder that many Americans no longer believe in the traditional manner of wealth building (i.e., husband works, wife stays home, retires with a pension) when they see how the traditional structure of "family" has blurred.

WHAT IS A PERSON TO DO?

Although the dynamics of "family" have changed, the fundamental basis of financial planning taught through the *Wealth Workout* program remain the same.

We will introduce you to three households, real people just like you, who have been intimidated and confused by the world of investments, people who juggle daily responsibilities and yet found the time to dispel the money myths by utilizing the tools of *Wealth Workout*. And you will see exceptional, real-world results! While our households are composed of real people, their names have been changed, and certain financial information has been modified in order to show the impact of all the principles we discuss in this book. These principles have evolved into what we now call the *Wealth Workout* program.

Learn, for example, how Linda and Michael—a dual-income couple in their 40s—emerged from a financially dysfunctional, debt-ridden lifestyle and moved on to the path to fiscal well-being and wealth accumulation. You'll discover how they slashed their expenses, utilized innovative financial strategies, and launched a systematic investment program designed to achieve the dual goals of a comfortable lifestyle and financial security.

Best of all, the techniques that guided and empowered Linda and Michael—as well as the other people you will meet in this book, including Chuck (a single 35 year old) and Pat and Ruth (a couple in their 50s), are all carefully explained and fully available to you.

As you advance through the program, you will realize a number of parallels between a successful physical fitness workout and a successful financial fitness workout:

PHYSICAL FITNESS		FINANCIAL FITNESS
Weight reduction	=	Expense reduction
Builds muscle	=	Builds wealth
Personal physical fitness trainer	=	Personal financial fitness trainer
Measurable results	=	Measurable results

You will notice that in each chapter we have provided worksheets to be completed during each weekly exercise. TEAR THEM

OUT. Use them as tools to record and personalize your progress. When you're finished, post them where you'll see them, using them for daily motivation and a reminder of your efforts.

As you advance through the program, utilize the full allotted time frame to finish each exercise. For example, as you work through **Week One: Setting Your Financial Goals,** use the entire week to thoughtfully complete the worksheets, filling in your personal goals and estimated costs to achieve them. Why start with goals? If you don't have goals, you won't be motivated to work out. What's more, these worksheets will become your benchmark for assessing your performance throughout the fitness program.

Week Two: Measuring Your Waste Line. During this week, you will conduct a fiscal exam of your current financial situation, including an honest review of your net worth and cash flow. You will evaluate everything you own and owe and through this process will find out exactly where you are on the road to achieving financial security. This is an ideal time to take advantage of the expertise of a personal money trainer. We'll tell you how to find one in this chapter.

Week Three: Your Personal Fitness Plan helps you develop your fiscal workout plan. Based on your age, income, and time horizon, this exercise will reveal how much money you must invest on a monthly basis to achieve your goals. The exercise will also explain the importance and potency of RATE OF RETURN and TIME on your ability to successfully complete your plan.

Weeks Four and Five: Cut the Fat begins by cutting unnecessary expenditures from your budget. You will be asked to eliminate all discretionary spending for a period of two weeks. Cold turkey! Feel free to call your personal money trainer for encouragement and advice.

As part of the process, we will reveal sources for budget cutting and strategies to reduce your debt. You will set guidelines for allocating the additional cash that's accumulated after trimming your budgetary waste line.

In keeping with your goal to reshape your fiscal body, you must understand that our *Wealth Workout* program goes far beyond cutting expenses. Expense-reduction strategies alone do not work. They must work in tandem with wealth-building activities.

Weeks Six and Seven: Pump It Up. Here you will begin to engage in wealth-building activities by first exploring investment options, such as mutual funds, that will give you an opportunity to change the shape of your fiscal body. These financial exercises have the capacity to reward you with increased financial resources to fund your dreams of a new home, advanced education, or a comfortable retirement.

Weeks Eight and Nine: Reward Yourself explores how to maintain a balanced investment diet that builds wealth through the years. You will learn four key investment strategies of a systematic investment plan: strategic asset allocation, diversification, dollar-cost averaging, and buy-hold. These four basic investment strategies are all you need to reward yourself with a lifetime of financial security.

Week Ten: Tax Attack will walk you through the wealth-building power of tax-wise investing, methods to counter the wealth-draining impact of Uncle Sam through options such as IRAs, 401(k)s, Keoghs, and tax-exempt mutual funds. By the time you reach the end of this chapter, you'll know how to incorporate these strategies into fitness portfolios that can provide the highest possible levels of after-tax returns.

Week Eleven: Protecting Your Gluteus Maximus reveals various ways to protect against events beyond your control that could jeopardize your *Wealth Workout* plan: life and disability insurance, long-term healthcare, and estate planning. You'll discover, through additional worksheets, what steps you must take to protect your assets so that you can maximize your family's financial well-being during your lifetime and after you pass away.

Week Twelve: Fitness for Life is perhaps the most important week of the plan because it stresses the important principles that are necessary for you to follow to remain financially fit for life. We discuss three areas that will directly impact your financial future and that you therefore must give thoughtful consideration to for the remainder of your life: discipline, long-term thinking, and maintenance.

The exercise concludes with a discussion of your seasonal evaluation worksheet, which monitors your progress throughout the year, and a discussion of the importance of your annual weigh-in review with your personal money trainer.

If you do not presently have a personal money trainer, give us a call at H.D. Vest Financial Services, 1-800-4-Wealth. H.D. Vest Financial Services was the first, and is the foremost, financial services firm serving the American investor through a network of tax and financial professionals. Since its inception in 1983, H.D. Vest's success in the financial services marketplace has been reflected in its growing representative base and the increasing number of clients it serves.

Thousands of professionals in all 50 states have joined H.D. Vest. They are independent practitioners who possess the highest professional qualifications: certified public accountants, enrolled agents, certified financial planners, tax attorneys, and public accountants. Using H.D. Vest's proven strategy of diversified mutual fund investing as their base, representatives work with their clients to produce comprehensive, personalized financial programs, encompassing securities, insurance, and professional portfolio management.

Note: Throughout this book, example returns illustrate various points. The most commonly used percentages are 6 percent and 10 percent. There is nothing magical or even significant about these numbers. They are simply convenient benchmarks. Actual returns on investment vehicles will vary and are greatly affected by risk, time, and economic cycles.

EXERCISE
one

BEFORE   AFTER

Week 1
SETTING YOUR FINANCIAL GOALS

SETTING YOUR FINANCIAL GOALS

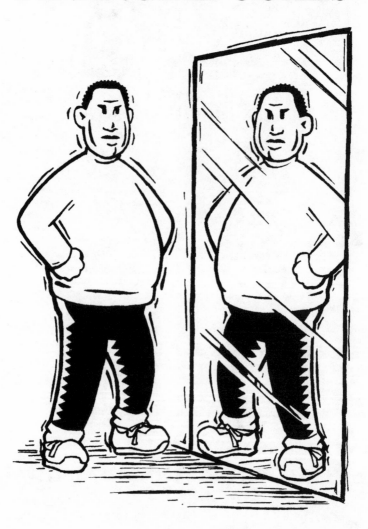

Week 1 Warm-Up Exercise:

1. Stand up straight in front of a full-length mirror with your hands firmly planted on your hips, knees slightly bent:
2. Stare directly into your eyes with a slightly tensed and furrowed brow.
3. Maintain full eye contact and loudly repeat three times, "I will establish and prioritize my goals." Repeat as necessary each morning throughout this week and record all results on this worksheet.

Financial Goals Worksheet
as of _____

Goals	Priority	Estimated Cost	Years to Goal
eliminate debt	1	$8,300	3 mos
save	1		
max contribution	1		
buy nice clothes	3		
charitable giving	2		
buy cottage on Vineyard	3	$450,000	10

EVERY RED, WHITE, AND BLUE WORKING
AMERICAN CAN ACHIEVE WEALTH

> **You must first identify your financial goals before you can begin to take charge of your financial dreams.**

Not by wishing, dreaming, or playing the powerball lottery, but by setting financial goals, having a burning desire to achieve them, and having a wealth-building system to guide him or her along the way.

Most of you are familiar with the diet and exercise programs that motivate you by presenting the infamous "before and after" pictures. You must do the same thing with this financial fitness program by first thoughtfully examining your financial present and then visualizing your financial future. Your end product will be a number of specific and attainable financial goals. These financial goals will become your motivational kick-start to begin this unique 90-day fitness program and, more importantly, to maintain it.

Achieving financial success will take discipline and effort, but IT WILL HAPPEN once you make the commitment and stay on track with your goals.

Give this process of identifying goals a great deal of thoughtful consideration: do not rush to judgment. Once identified, it is critical that you QUANTIFY each financial goal with a specific dollar amount and time frame. Identification without quantification becomes pie in the sky.

> **Unhappiness is in not knowing what we want and killing ourselves to get it.**
>
> *Don Herold*

When establishing goals, BE REALISTIC about what you really want to achieve—not what you would accept as a compromise. For example, if your goal is to buy a turn-of-the-century historical Dutch colonial home, don't settle for a cookie cutter tract home simply because you made a snap conclusion that your financial situation will not allow for the mortgage payment . . . economic situations change.

It is also imperative that you REMOVE CONFLICTS that stand in the way of your goals. (No, we do not mean you should sell the kids.) For instance, setting a goal to lose 30 pounds while continuing to consume high-fat drinks, meals, and desserts every evening with your spouse or friends is a conflict. If you are serious about weight loss, you must cut back the fat in your diet.

> **What I have said, that I will bring about, what I have planned, that I will do.**
>
> *Isaiah 46:11*

In addition, the *Wealth Workout* program requires you to CUT BACK ON YOUR EXPENSES.

Your success at reaching your financial goals through the *Wealth Workout* program will be in direct proportion to the extent of your desire and determination. But whatever you do, DON'T GET DISCOURAGED.

THE KEY HERE IS TO THINK ABOUT YOUR GOALS IN RELATION TO YOUR LIFESTYLE.

You will without a doubt, make adjustments and sacrifices to achieve your financial goals, but it doesn't mean that you can't have fun and reap the rewards along the way!

Accomplishing your major goals will take time and effort. However, writing them down will make them real and attainable.

After you quantify, prioritize, and begin to take action on your goals, you will begin to see POSITIVE RESULTS rather quickly. Your mailbox may begin to thin out as a result of fewer bills, and your wallet may begin to bulge with newfound strength.

THREE SUCCESS STORIES

To illustrate the STRENGTH AND POWER of our fitness program, we invite you to join the progress of three American households who in the mid-80s learned the benefits of applying the principles of the *Wealth Workout* program. Their profiles are similar to millions of American families. They have successfully completed the *Wealth Workout* program and are now on their way to becoming financially fit for life.

Each household had their own unique set of financial circumstances, and each could relate to some of these widely held beliefs shared by many Americans:

1. Each lived paycheck to paycheck, hand to mouth.
2. They did not believe they earned enough to invest.
3. They did not know how to plan for financial fitness.
4. They were financially out of shape.

Let's meet each of them now.

Chuck

Chuck was a typical, young, struggling single when he entered the *Wealth Workout* program. He was 35 years old, rented a modest apartment, drove an import, and drove his girlfriend nuts with sports statistics. He earned $37,500 a year as a machine operator at the local paper mill and spent nearly every cent on . . . something, but he could never quantify the "what" and "where" of it all.

Chuck was clueless about the process of saving and investing until he learned about the principles of the *Wealth Workout* program. He had no written goals. He rarely thought about his future financial security because in his mind he wasn't making the "big bucks" to even consider such an abstract concept as "wealth." He didn't have an investment strategy but did manage to tuck away $1,000 per year in his savings account.

Linda and Michael

Linda and her husband Michael were both 40 years old. Linda held an executive position with a large, well-established company that manufactured computer chips. Michael was self-employed as a bankruptcy consultant. They earned a combined salary of $100,000, which came in handy in supporting the expensive tastes of two children in high school.

Despite their income, Michael and Linda were as clueless as Chuck in terms of establishing a savings or investment plan, except for the amounts directed to an IRA. Although their income placed them in the upper 5 percent of all American wage earners, Michael and Linda were deeply in debt.

They were a financially dysfunctional mess. They had 10 credit cards—EACH—all nearly maxed to the limits, with a balance in excess of $10,000. They drove two leased imports and carried a huge mortgage on their home. You guessed it, they were spinning out of control.

Pat and Ruth

 Pat and Ruth were both 50 and had the wonder years of raising three children behind them. However, they were also members of an exploding part of our society that is assuming an ever-larger financial role for elder care, in this case, spending out-of-pocket cash to help care for Pat's 70-year-old father, who had had a stroke. Over the years, they managed to save approximately $150,000, parking all of it in CDs at their local bank. Pat's income totalled $75,000 per year. Ruth did not work outside the home.

They owned their home free and clear of any mortgage, and their late-model cars were fully paid for. So what was wrong with their picture? How were they financially threatened? In the short term, life for Pat and Ruth was relatively secure; in the long term, life could easily have meant a part-time job as a security guard at the local mall and macaroni and cheese for dinner if they were not willing to become more aggressive with their savings. Their greatest risk was that they may outlive their money.

Pat and Ruth desperately needed to create a financial plan that would do two things:

1. Make up for low returns over the years by investing a portion of their holdings in growth assets.

2. Build an elder care fund that would be available to help Pat's father without draining their retirement fund.

ESTABLISHING GOALS

Upon committing to enter into this program, all three households had to identify and quantify their goals. Each admitted that this task was the most difficult reality check of the program, but it also turned out to be the most beneficial. Let's take a look at their financial goals and learn how the exercise helped each of them define their own personalized wealth-building strategy.

─────────────────| Do This Now |─────────────────

This is your cue to tear out the Financial Goals Worksheet at the front of this chapter and begin the thoughtful process of establishing your financial goals.

After we examine the following goals of our three households, we will show you how to calculate what you will need to complete your first exercise to true financial fitness and health.

Chuck: Wealth Workout Financial Goals Worksheet

Goal	Priority	Estimated Cost	Years to Goal
Emergency fund	1	$ 15,000	3
New furniture	2	10,000	3
New car	3	10,000	5
Condo	4	100,000	10
Retirement	5	1,137,000	30

Linda and Michael: Wealth Workout Financial Goals Worksheet

Goal	Priority	Estimated Cost	Years to Goal
Pay credit cards	1	$ 10,000	2
Emergency fund	2	36,000	5
Educational fund	3		
Eric		47,300	3

Brad		50,100	4
Buy cars	4	20,000	5
Buy boat	5	80,000	10
Retirement	6	2,493,000	25

Pat and Ruth: Wealth Workout Financial Goals Worksheet

Goal	Priority	Estimated Cost	Years to Goal
Elder care	1	$ 50,000	5
New car	2	15,000	3
Vacation home	3	80,000	5
Retirement	4	1,263,000	15

Let's talk briefly about MAJOR FINANCIAL GOALS and how to calculate each in order for you to complete this workout.

While you can have numerous financial goals, WE RECOMMEND THAT YOU KEEP YOUR GOALS TO NO MORE THAN SIX; the fewer the better. This will enable you to focus on your most burning desires and therefore increase the probability of achieving them.

PRIORITIZING YOUR GOALS

It is critical that you review each of the following goals to determine how important they are to you. Use your Financial Goals Worksheet not only to list your goals but to prioritize them—from highest to lowest. Prioritizing will help you determine the order in which to pursue each goal.

Seven Common Goals

These are the goals that are common to most working Americans:

1. Eliminating debt.
2. Establishing an emergency fund.
3. Making large consumer-good purchases.
4. Purchasing a home.
5. Educational funding.

6. Secure retirement.

An additional goal on the fast-track to becoming common:

7. Elder care funding.

Let's take a closer look at each one.

CALCULATING YOUR FINANCIAL GOALS

Eliminating Debt

It has been reported that in the mid-1990s total outstanding credit balances on the popular Mastercard and Visa cards alone are exceeding $ 197 billion dollars, yes, that's BILLION.

———————————————⊣ Do This Now ⊢———————————————

So, let's haul out your credit card statements and add up the balances to learn how much of this debt is yours. Upon doing so, enter the total figure on your worksheet.

Credit cards can be a convenience but can also be a financial form of cancer, particularly when balances start to mount and interest charges accrue. If you related to the financial perils of Michael and Linda, our best advice is to SNIP, SNIP, SNIP the bulk of your cards. Keep only those cards you may need in case of an emergency.

The chances of eliminating your spiraling debt will be enhanced by eliminating the opportunity to charge by plastic.

For the surviving one or two cards, attempt to PAY OFF THE BALANCES in full on a monthly basis. If carrying a balance is unavoidable, it is important to know the terms of the card such as the rate and annual fee.

Emergency Fund

Three months of net take-home income was the rule of thumb advocated by financial planners for years when it came to building a family emergency fund. However, times have changed, and the thumb has grown to six months.

Why the change? Secure jobs may well be history, and having more cash to cope with during times of uncertainty is the safest way to cover yourself. (Building a fund to upgrade your career skills is covered in our discussion of educational funding.)

---------------| **Do This Now** |---------------

How large of a fund will you need to build? Perform the following simple multiplication by first inserting your net monthly household take-home pay on the blank line under the column "You".

	Chuck	Linda and Michael	You
Monthly take-home pay	$2,500	$6,000	$ *2800*
Times 6	X 6	X 6	X 6
Emergency funds needed	$15,000	$36,000	$ *168 00*

RECORD THE FIGURE ON YOUR FINANCIAL GOALS WORKSHEET.

Large Purchases

A number of factors come into play when estimating the cost of a large, major purchase, be it furniture, a boat, a vacation home, or a car. For the sake of this exercise, let us consider a large purchase as a tangible asset that you are unable to purchase with walking-around money and is expected to last a number of years.

While we encourage you to SAVE FOR LARGE PURCHASES to avoid debt, we also realize that it may not always be practical to pay cash. Therefore, it is safe to assume that most large purchases are financed. Both cash and debt options will be explored in Week 3.

---------------| **Do This Now** |---------------

For now, ESTIMATE the purchase price of any large purchases you wish to make and list each on the Financial Goals Worksheet.

Home Purchase

According to the US Bureau of Labor Statistics, in 1994 skin-flints and spendthrifts alike shelled out on average 32 percent of their budget on the purchase and maintenance of a home.

Lenders have been waging a mortgage war, dropping down-payment requirements on some mortgages from 10 percent to 5 percent.

However, before you slice a piece of the American pie, it is advisable that you deliberately open your mind to the economic reality of owning your own home by asking yourself questions such as these:

- What can I afford?

- Should I buy new or old?

- How much of a down payment should I make?

- What is the real cost of ownership?

Owning a home may or may not be a good investment, but it is part of the American dream. So, if you fully understand that ownership will take time, energy, and money; that home repairs and upkeep will be costly; that you will become your own landlord, garbage collector, and repairman, it is critical for you to calculate the size of your down payment in order to work it into your *Wealth Workout* financial plan.

THE DOWN PAYMENT SHOULD BE AS LOW AS YOU CAN POSSIBLY ARRANGE in your residential market of choice. Why? The strongest reason is that you will free up additional funds to invest toward your other financial goals. This is true if your investments can outperform your mortgage rate. Also, be aware that you may have to pay private mortgage insurance if your mortgage is greater than 80 percent of the value of your home.

For example, Chuck wants to buy a condo in 10 years and thinks it will cost $100,000. Will he be able to afford it based on his current financial situation ?

In Week 3, we will spend more time on this calculation, to include how much house you and Chuck each can afford and how much money you will need for the house you want.

─────────────────┤ Do This Now ├─────────────────

For now, we want you to list on your Financial Goals Worksheet what you estimate the house you want will cost.

Educational Funding

Second only to planning for your own retirement, educational funding may well be the largest financial challenge that you face. THE KEY TO SUCCESSFULLY SAVING ENOUGH GREENBACKS FOR A FOUR-YEAR COLLEGE DEGREE IS TO BEGIN EARLY.

THE SOONER YOU DEVELOP A SYSTEMATIC INVEST-MENT PLAN, THE MORE TIME YOU WILL HAVE TO ACCU-MULATE THE NECESSARY FUNDS. A college education is a good investment. A US Census Bureau report emphasizes that college graduates outearn those with high school diplomas by more than $360,000 over the course of a normal working lifetime.

> **Education's purpose is to replace an empty mind with an open one.**
> *Malcolm Forbes*

Costs will vary according to the type of institution of higher learning, but Table 1–1 will show you a very simple method to determine the necessary funds required of you based upon the number of years to go before your child attends college.

Linda and Michael had two children: Eric, who would enter college in three years and Brad, who would enter in four. Therefore, they would need to save $47,300 in three years for Eric and $50,100 in four years for Brad. (One small hint: These guys were in trouble.)

As a footnote, when saving money for education, you may want to consider a Uniform Gift to Minors Act (UGMA) account. Funds are placed in a trust for the benefit of a child. Funds accumulating in the trust are taxed at the minor's tax rate rather than the parent's higher rate. This tax break is limited to $1,200 of income per year for children under age 14; income in excess of

$1,200 in any given year is taxed at the parent's tax rate. The downside to a UGMA is that the child receives all of the trust assets at age of majority (usually 18) and can do anything he or she wishes with the funds.

—————————————⊣ **Do This Now** ⊢———————————————

Enter the appropriate amount(s) for your children based on the number of years until college and then enter the amounts on your Financial Goals Worksheet.

TABLE 1-1:   Funds Needed for College/Advanced Education

Years to College	Public	Private	Linda and Michael	You
1	$ 42,100	87,700		
2	44,600	93,000		
3	47,300	98,600	47,300	
4	50,100	104,500	50,100	
5	53,100	110,700		
6	56,300	117,400		
7	59,700	124,400		
8	63,300	131,900		
9	67,100	139,800		
10	71,100	148,200		
11	75,400	157,100		
12	79,900	166,500		
13	84,700	176,500		
14	89,800	187,100		
15	95,200	198,300		
16	100,900	210,200		
17	106,900	222,800		
18	113,300	236,200		

Assumes a 6% annual increase in cost, based on 1993–94 academic year.

Adult Education

In the early 1990s, American businesses went on the equivalent of a liquid fast, shedding thousands and thousands of jobs much like dieters peel off excess pounds. Many of these jobs will never return. This job-shedding process was, and remains, part of a fundamental employment shift in the United States toward service industries.

According to the Bureau of Labor Statistics, job advancement opportunities through the year 2005 will be best for those with the most education and training. The higher the education level, the greater the annual income and the greater the potential for earnings over a lifetime. Adults now have an ever-increasing opportunity to obtain designations, certifications, and advanced degrees from nontraditional sources.

Pursuing these opportunities will increase their marketability and improve their ability to change careers without the costly and timely requirements demanded from the traditional educational system. You should consider education as an ongoing investment over the course of your lifetime and plan to allocate part of your savings/earnings to this goal.

Retirement

All of us have been blitzed with media messages telling us that the likelihood of living to an older age is increasing, that the average life expectancy in the United States is now nearly 80 years of age!

Many of us will need retirement income for 20 years or more, equal to 80 percent of our current income, adjusted, of course, for inflation. You should be asking yourself, "HOW MUCH MONEY WILL I NEED?"

The answer to this question is variable, based upon a number of issues. However, one thing is certain: The sooner you learn the answer, the better off you will be when you do retire.

For the vast majority of us, retirement will not be totally financed by Social Security and pension checks. This makes planning for retirement even more difficult, like trying to hit a moving target while blindfolded or putting together a jigsaw puzzle without all of the pieces.

Sources of Retirement Income

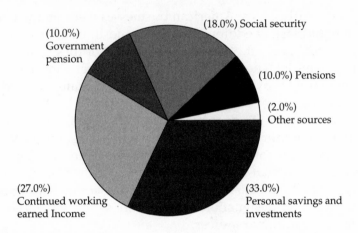

(10.0%)
Government
pension

(18.0%) Social security

(10.0%) Pensions

(2.0%)
Other sources

(27.0%)
Continued working
earned Income

(33.0%)
Personal savings and
investments

Source: U.S. Department of Health and Human Services, 1992.

An article in *The Wall Street Journal* (Alan L. Otten, March 24, 1995) reported that Americans admit they could cut back spending to save more for retirement; but, according to survey results, comparatively few intend to do so. Talk about your head in the sand!

It seems that many people have justified their unwillingness to cut back by simply redefining or expanding their definition of *basics* and *necessities*. How will basics and necessities be expanded in retirement? Who do these people expect will pay for their retirement expansion? What are they thinking?

Most respondents to the survey agreed that spending on clothing or travel was "essential" to their standard of living, areas in which they are no longer willing to consider pulling back. These are the same people who are barely able to save 4 percent of their annual income. One visit to a nursing care facility will slap anyone into reality that one is not able to "redefine" retirement. When you're old, you're old; basics and necessities will be out the window for those who are not financially prepared.

Regardless of how you personally view the retirement game, the most important thing to understand is that NOW IS THE TIME TO TAKE ACTION.

Table 1–2 on page 18 will help you estimate the amount of money you may need to finance your current standard of living in retirement.

The amounts reflected in this table were calculated assuming you would earn a 10 percent rate of return on your investments during retirement, that you would retire at age 65, and that you will live until age 85.

Of course, the numbers may not accurately reflect your individual situation, but that's OK because at this point we are only asking you to estimate. For example, your rate of return could be lower, inflation higher, and the number of years in retirement longer. Later in the book, we will show you how to adjust these assumptions more specifically to your personal circumstances.

All you have to do now is find the annual income you desire at retirement across the horizontal axis of Table 1–2 and years to retire listed down the vertical axis. To calculate the annual income you desire, follow the simple example below. Eighty percent of your current income is the general rule of thumb used to estimate the amount of annual income needed in retirement. You can safely assume your expenses will be less in retirement—no kids, home paid for, and so on. On the other hand, you don't want to reduce your current standard of living—that would be too great a sacrifice when you are supposed to be enjoying your golden years.

	Chuck	Linda and Michael	Pat and Ruth	You
Annual income	$ 37,500	$ 100,000	$ 75,000	
	X 80%	X 80%	X 80%	
Retirement income	30,000	80,000	60,000	
Funds needed at retirement (from Table 1–2)	$ 1,137,000	$ 2,493,000	$1,263,000	

RECORD THE FIGURE ON YOUR FINANCIAL GOALS WORKSHEET

Elder Care Funding

According to the US Census Bureau, today's 65 year old can look forward to another 17.6 years of sunrises and sunsets. The

TABLE 1-2:   Lump Sum Needed to Provide Income Needs at Retirement

Estimated Annual Income Needed (in today's dollars)

Years to Retirement	$10,000	$20,000	$30,000	$40,000	$50,000
45	683,000	1,365,000	2,048,000	2,731,000	3,413,000
42	607,000	1,214,000	1,821,000	2,428,000	3,035,000
40	561,000	1,112,000	1,683,000	2,244,000	2,806,000
37	499,000	998,000	1,497,000	1,995,000	2,494,000
35	461,000	922,000	1,384,000	1,845,000	2,306,000
32	410,000	820,000	1,230,000	1,640,000	2,050,000
30	379,000	758,000	1,137,000	1,516,000	1,895,000
27	337,000	674,000	1,011,000	1,348,000	1,685,000
25	312,000	623,000	935,000	1,246,000	1,558,000
22	277,000	554,000	831,000	1,108,000	1,385,000
20	256,000	512,000	768,000	1,024,000	1,280,000
17	228,000	455,000	683,000	911,000	1,138,000
15	210,000	421,000	631,000	842,000	1,052,000
12	187,000	374,000	561,000	749,000	936,000
10	173,000	346,000	519,000	692,000	865,000
7	154,000	308,000	461,000	615,000	769,000
5	142,000	284,000	427,000	569,000	711,000

children of this growing demographic shift can also look forward to the inevitable illness that will face these aging Americans.

CARING FOR AN ILL PARENT WILL COST YOU DEARLY IF YOU ARE NOT FINANCIALLY PREPARED. Few of us are prepared for the disruptive calamity of elder care illness. Pat and Ruth were not emotionally prepared for the telephone call that Pat's father had suffered a stroke and was hospitalized. Every aspect of their lives changed for the next six months, including Pat's work schedule and the cash drain from their savings

TABLE 1–2: (concluded)

Years to Retirement	Estimated Annual Income Needed (in today's dollars)				
	$60,000	$70,000	$80,000	$90,000	$100,000
45	4,096,000	4,779,000	5,462,000	6,144,000	6,827,000
42	3,642,000	4,249,000	4,856,000	5,462,000	6,069,000
40	3,367,000	3,928,000	4.489,000	5,050,000	5,611,000
37	2,993,000	3,492,000	3,991,000	4,490,000	4,989,000
35	2,767,000	3,229,000	3,690,000	4,151,000	4,612,000
32	2,460,000	2,870,000	3,280,000	3,690,000	4,100,000
30	2,275,000	2,654,000	3,033,000	3,442,000	3,791,000
27	2,022,000	2,359,000	2,696,000	3,033,000	3,370,000
25	1,869,000	2,181,000	2,493,000	2,804,000	3,116,000
22	1,662,000	1,939,000	2,216,000	2,493,000	2,770,000
20	1,537,000	1,793,000	2,049,000	2,305,000	2,561,000
17	1,366,000	1,594,000	1,821,000	2,049,000	2,277,000
15	1,263,000	1,473,000	1,684,000	1,894,000	2,105,000
12	1,123,000	1,310,000	1,497,000	1,684,000	1,871,000
10	1,038,000	1,211,000	1,384,000	1,557,000	1,730,000
7	923,000	1,077,000	1,230,000	1,384,000	1,538,000
5	853,000	995,000	1,138,000	1,280,000	1,422,000

Assuming 4% inflation, and assuming funds will earn 10% from date of retirement at age 65. Assumes life expectancy of 20 years after retirement. Rounded to the nearest thousand. Source: H.D. Vest Financial Services

account to pay for a hotel room and meals in close proximity to the hospital.

For the long term, elder care funding includes careful consideration of financing adult day care as well as nursing home care. Pat and Ruth were convinced that in order to insulate their retirement money they needed to establish elder funding as their number one priority. They estimated they would need to spend $10,000 per year for at least five years if Pat's dad should have to go to a nursing home. Therefore, they set a goal of $50,000.

CONGRATULATIONS!

Over the past week, you have successfully identified, quantified, and prioritized the goals that are most important to your future.

In the coming weeks as you continue through each workout, you will be asked to refer back to these goals in order to learn the most efficient way to achieve them.

As a result of the decisions you will make throughout this process, it may be necessary for you to reprioritize one goal over another or perhaps increase or decrease the necessary time frame to achieve a specific goal. No matter what the adjustment may be, it is of utmost importance that you remain FOCUSED and FLEXIBLE.

THE NEXT 83 DAYS WILL BE THE MOST IMPORTANT 83 DAYS OF YOUR LIFE. You will begin to transition your finances, reinforcing your foundation for financial security. It doesn't matter who you are, how much income you earn, or how much you owe, you CAN reach the goals you set.

Stay tuned . . . because you are just getting started! If you really, we mean REALLY, want that new home, college for your kids, or a secure retirement, you are ready to go to Week 2: Measuring Your Waste Line.

EXERCISE

two

Week 2
MEASURING YOUR WASTE LINE

MEASURING YOUR
WASTE LINE

Week 2 Warm-Up Exercise:

1. Firmly grasp your cardboard box, marked "Important Papers."
2. In one fluid gesture, tilt the box upside down, dispensing all receipts and records (preferably upon a desk or kitchen table).
3. With concentrated gaze, begin to firmly grasp each receipt and fondly recall how your spending habits have been paved with good intentions. Conduct multiple repetitions of step three, discussing openly with your spouse (if applicable).

Net Worth Worksheet
as of _____

What You Own	What You Owe
Liquid Assets:	**Liabilities:**
Checking accounts _____	Credit card balances *$5,000*
Savings accounts *$25,00*	Car loans _____
Money market accounts *$500*	Education loans _____
Cash value— life insurance _____	Mortgage *$150,000* ~~$223,00~~
Other _____	Other *2,000*
Total _____	Total *$9,000*
Investment Assets:	
Mutual funds *$20,000*	
Stocks _____	
Bonds _____	
CDs _____	
IRA *$2,000*	
401(k) *$25,000*	
Pension plan _____	
Other _____	
Total _____	

Net Worth Worksheet
as of _____

What You Own
Personal Assets:
Home $230,000
Other property   _____
Automobiles   _____
Jewelry/art $4,000
Household $8,000
Other   _____
   Total   242,000

Total assets   (+) _____
Minus liabilities (–) _____
Net worth   (=) _____

Cash Flow Worksheet
as of_____

What You Earned (Income)	Per Month	Per Year
Household wages and salaries	_____	$65,000
Dividends and interest	_____	_____
Annuities and pensions	_____	_____
Social Security	_____	_____
Tips and commissions	_____	_____
Other _____	_____	_____
Total	_____	_____

What You Spent (Expenses)
Fixed expenses:

	Per Month	Per Year
Taxes	_____	_____
Mortgage or rent	_____	_____
Utilities	_____	_____
Child care	_____	_____
Phone	_____	_____
Other fixed	_____	_____
Loan and debt payments:		
Car	_____	_____
Credit cards	_____	_____

Cash Flow Worksheet
as of _____

What You Spent (Expenses)	Per Month	Per Year
Other debt payments	_____	_____
Variable expenses:		
Food	_____	_____
Medical	_____	_____
Clothing	_____	_____
Tuition/education	_____	_____
Homeowner insurance	_____	_____
Auto insurance	_____	_____
Home maintenance	_____	_____
Auto maintenance	_____	_____
Hobbies	_____	_____
Entertainment	_____	_____
Restaurants	_____	_____
Vacations	_____	_____
Club memberships	_____	_____
Gifts	_____	_____
Charitable donations	_____	_____
Dry cleaning	_____	_____
Life and disability insurance	_____	_____
Unaccounted for expenses	_____	_____
Total expenses	_____	_____
Income – expenses = Level of insanity	═══════	═══════

What You Invested (Investments and Savings)

	Per Month	Per Year
IRA	_____	_____
401(k)	_____	_____
Other	_____	_____
Total	═══════	═══════

The chairman of the U.S. Federal Reserve Board recently remarked that he believes American households, and the United States as a country, are experiencing a "PERSISTENT ACCOUNT IMBALANCE" (i.e., no savings and high deficits). In other words, most Americans are in deep do-do.

> **Money isn't everything as long as you have enough.**
>
> *Malcolm Forbes*

Why is this a persistent condition? Why do so many people feel such a loss of control over their money? Bookstores are stocked to the rafters with financial expert books that explain technical methods to save and invest for a secure financial future.

WHY DOES IT APPEAR THAT WALL STREET HAS FAILED MAIN STREET? Because the material is far too complex and confusing for the average investment-inclined American who is growing increasingly frightened by a cloudy and fast-approaching future. The public is so turned off by the technical hype that they completely ignore it.

Wealth Workout puts a stop to the technical theories, charts, and graphs by PLACING YOU IN CHARGE with a down-to-earth approach to strategies that will lead you to financial success!

The strategy for the next seven days is to MEASURE YOUR WASTE LINE by doing your gut-level best to calculate your current net worth and current cash flow.

As you have undoubtedly thumbed through a number of pages in this book to get a feel for the content and what is expected of you throughout the 90-day workout, you have probably realized that much of what we plan to ask of you will not be a walk in the park.

Is this exercise strict, rigid, and perhaps a bit intimidating? To those of you who are new investors, the answer is probably yes. It certainly was a resounding yes for Michael and Linda, the king and queen of excess. Michael's definition of *cash flow* was limited to how quickly the ATM machine pumped out money. Linda thought that net worth was some "values thing."

You should take heart in knowing that a good old-fashioned and disciplined approach to completing this exercise will prove to you that your Waste Line Workout is the most ENLIGHTENING of all *Wealth Workout* exercises.

─────────────────┤ Do This Now ├─────────────────

Before we get underway, let's do some housekeeping by first removing the Cash Flow and Net Worth Worksheets at the beginning of this chapter.

─────────────────┤ Do This Now ├─────────────────

Also, be certain that you have recovered all known boxes of important papers squirreled away around your home. This will provide you with easy access to specific numbers when filling in the blanks of your worksheets.

If you are a normal, hard-working American trying to squeeze 25 hours out of a 24 hour day, your records are probably a scattered mess . . . not to worry. At the end of this chapter, you will find a number of specific tips on how to better organize your finance-related records.

Before you begin this eye-popping mental odyssey, it is important, no, IT IS *CRITICAL* THAT YOU UNDERSTAND HOW IMPORTANT IT IS TO CONDUCT A THOROUGH, HONEST, AND PERSONAL AUDIT (NET WORTH/CASH FLOW EXAM) OF YOUR PRESENT FINANCIAL CONDITION *BEFORE* YOU CAN PERSONALIZE YOUR FUTURE FINANCIAL PLAN.

Most of us understand that before beginning any type of aggressive physical exercise program or event, it is highly recommended to visit the family doctor for a complete physical exam. After all, anyone with half a brain would not jump into the Boston Marathon without knowing if they were a candidate for cardiac arrest.

In similar fashion, examining your net worth and cash flow is a complete fiscal exam of your current financial condition, the most critical time for you to poke your wallet and stick out your financial tongue. This workout will prepare you to jump into and run the financial marathon of your life.

This week would also be the perfect time to seek out professional advice from an accountant or financial planner, your personal money trainer. If you do not have a relationship with an accountant or financial planner, we will discuss the ins and outs of finding one at the end of this exercise.

This exercise will cause you to get a grip on your finances. It is not intended to steal from you the freedom of how you choose to spend your money but, quite the contrary, is intended to reveal to you new choices, new thoughts, and new opportunities on how to invest your money for the future rather than throwing it away today.

> **Real generosity toward the future lies in giving all to the present.**
>
> *Camus*

Let's not kid ourselves at this point: This exercise may get ugly, but the effort will reward you with a sense of CONTROL, BALANCE, AND DIRECTION over the ins and outs of your money. You will rise every morning and go to sleep every night with the confidence that you and your family are ever more secure from financial disaster.

It will also reveal a clear picture of your attitude toward money and CREATE A POSITIVE ATTITUDE ABOUT YOURSELF.

Note the equation at the bottom of your Cash Flow Worksheet: "Income – Expenses = LEVEL OF INSANITY."

Quite simply, your family finances can drive you nuts! So what else is new? Completing this exercise will put some sanity into your financial life.

Chuck, like most of us, learned the knocks of finance the hard way: Living paycheck to paycheck, he was always faced with more days in the month than dollars. However, not only was his financial situation driving him nuts, but the demands of his job as a machine operator was also driving him bonkers; he was definitely in need of some control, balance, and direction in his life.

Linda and Michael needed to face reality very quickly and start thinking about tomorrow, which of course they did after they saw where they were spending their money and on what.

Pat and Ruth were in pretty good shape. They had excess cash for travel, hobbies, and abundant gifts for their children and family.

Let's take a look at how all three of these wealth wannabies calculated their net worth and cash flow.

Net Worth Worksheet

	Chuck	Linda and Michael	Pat and Ruth
What You Own			
Liquid Assets:			
Checking accounts	$ 2,000	$ 1,000	$ 5,000
Savings accounts	1,000		20,000
Cash value—life insurance			5,000
Total	3,000	1,000	30,000
Investment Assets:			
CDs			150,000
IRA		20,000	
Savings account	10,000		
Total	10,000	20,000	150,000
Personal Assets:			
Home		150,000	85,000
Automobiles	4,000	30,000	15,000
Household	6,000	30,000	30,000
Total	10,000	210,000	130,000
Total assets	23,000	231,000	310,000
What You Owe			
Liabilities:			
Credit cards	500	10,000	
Car loans		30,000	
Mortgage		125,000	
Total liabilities	500	165,000	0
Net worth	$ 22,500	$ 66,000	$ 310,000

Annual Cash Flow Worksheet

	Chuck	Linda and Michael	Pat and Ruth
Income:			
Household wages and salaries	$ 37,500	$ 100,000	$ 75,000
Dividends and interest	50	0	8,500
Total income	$ 37,550	$ 100,000	$ 83,500
Expenses:			
Fixed expenses:			
Taxes (FICA, fed, state, local, property)	10,400	32,150	30,000
Mortgage or rent	6,600	12,000	0
Utilities	600	1,600	1,200
Telephone	600	1,200	2,400
Total fixed	$ 18,200	$ 46,950	$ 33,600
Loan and Debt Payments:			
Car	0	8,400	0
Variable Expenses:			
Food	4,800	7,200	6,000
Medical	500	1,250	2,000
Clothing	2,000	4,000	4,000
Homeowners insurance	0	750	500
Auto insurance	850	1,250	1,000
Home maintenance	0	1,200	1,200
Auto maintenance	1,000	2,000	1,500
Entertainment	2,000	1,800	500
Restaurants	2,400	2,600	1,200
Vacations	2,000	6,600	5,000
Club memberships	0	600	0
Gifts	2,000	9,000	10,000
Dry cleaning	600	1,200	600
Life insurance	0	0	4,400
Total variable	18,150	39,450	37,900
Total expenses	36,350	94,800	71,500
Income – Expenses = Level of Insanity	$ 1,000	$ 5,200	$ 12,000
Investments and Savings:			
IRA	0	4,000	0
Savings account/CDs	1,000	0	12,000
Total investments & savings	$ 1,000	$ 4,000	$ 12,000

This Waste Line exercise will give you, as it gave all of our families, an opportunity to arrive at your "financial set point" or "balance," just as many dieters and exercise enthusiasts arrive at their set points of weight and fitness.

For those of you unfamiliar with the concept, our bodies tend to return to a set weight; that is, if we diet with discipline we lose weight, but once dieting is discontinued we return to our original weight. Conversely, if we splurge and gain weight, returning to normal eating will result in our gravitating toward our original weight.

In effect, the set point concept strikes a balance—whether it involves muscle or, in our case money—that signals a status quo and middle-of-the-road wholeness to the imbalance of life.

In your personal case, THIS FINANCIAL EXERCISE WILL SHOW YOU THE BALANCE OF HOW MUCH YOU OWN AND HOW MUCH YOU OWE, giving you a point of reference upon which to begin to plan and build a solid financial plan.

Upon examining the Net Worth and Cash Flow Worksheets, you will notice that each requires a great deal of information from your personal records, some of it quite detailed. Because of this requirement for vast amounts of data, it is extremely important that you not only commence this exercise as soon as possible but that you remain steadfast and disciplined in completing it.

TIME IS OF THE ESSENCE HERE. And as all of us know, time is totally irreplaceable and without substitute.

CALCULATING NET WORTH AND CASH FLOW

———————————| Do This Now |———————————

Let's take a closer look at each worksheet, beginning with the first page, which calculates your Net Worth.

It should make you feel better to know that a number of controllable and uncontrollable factors affect your net worth, factors such as the behavior and condition of the stock market.

Other factors are more genetic and far more personal, such as those that involve your age and your parents. Who would have thought when you were 16 that 20–30 years down the road your parents would continue to affect your life? (Some of us thought we were free from parental influence when we passed our driver's test.)

Medical advances and changing lifestyles are keeping more people living through midlife and on into old age, making elder care a potentially huge uncontrollable factor that is affecting or may affect your net worth. Have you missed work lately to care for an aged parent? How much of your income is supporting a parent's long-term care?

As we discussed in Week 1, these two questions are beginning to move to the front burner of financial planning as the number of aging parents per adult child is projected to nearly double by the year 2030, with families providing 80 percent of needed long-term care.

For most of you, another huge factor that can affect your net worth is children. How many do you have?

Those cute little bundle of joy pip-squeaks will cost you upwards of $500,000 *each* to raise from the delivery room through college graduation. American teens spent an estimated $99 billion in 1994! (Where do you think they got the money?)

The successful management of your marriage, career, and health is to a large extent "controllable"—this exercise will add to the list successful management of your finances in terms of how it also impacts your net worth. The obvious incentive here is to have a blissful relationship (with a working partner), a fast-track career, and a vibrant, healthy body. In terms of taking control over the management of your financial destiny, this exercise separates the wheat from the chaff, the good from the bad.

As you prepare to fill in the blanks of your Net Worth Worksheet, keep in mind that you want to be as *specific* as possible with each line-item figure.

Regarding your liquid assets, liabilities, and investment assets, use the most recent balance of any subcategory that provides you with a monthly or quarterly statement, such as your money market account, credit card, or certificate of deposit.

If you are beginning this *Wealth Workout* program in between interest-bearing statement dates, forget about trying to prorate x days of interest to your account but do congratulate yourself with a shiny star on the forehead for considering the effort.

A FEW TIPS ON CALCULATING THE VALUE OF YOUR PER-SONAL ASSETS:

- The figure for your home should reflect a realistic price that you would receive if you sold your home *today*. Without calling a realtor for comparable pricing, take a look around your neighborhood; someone is bound to have a home for sale. The sales price can usually be found in your local newspaper real estate section. Or simply call the listing agent and ask for the price.

- Other property could be considered real or personal property, such as a vacation home at the lake, a sailboat, or perhaps a travel trailer. As with your home, do your best to arrive at the realistic fair market value.

- The value of your automobile can be easily found by comparisons of similar models for sale in your local newspaper.

- The value of jewelry, art, and household items is largely subjective unless you can support specific purchases with receipts.

Following the completion of this worksheet, you will be in a position to learn how much you are worth. Simply subtract your total liabilities (what you owe) from your total assets (what you own), and voila, you have NET WORTH!

CONGRATULATIONS!

You have just completed the first half of the most difficult phase of financial planning—PULLING TOGETHER THE NUMBERS—an exercise that most Americans will never learn or take the time to do.

If your net worth figure is positive, you should be proud of yourself because it represents the positive decisions you have thus far made in your life to enhance your financial position.

———————————————┤ Do This Now ├———————————————

You are now in a position to attack page two of your exercise worksheet: CASH FLOW.

This phase of your workout must be undertaken with greater detail because it involves examining a number of areas where you *know* you are spending hard-earned dollars, but you can't quite put your finger on the hole: areas of discretionary spending where you throw around your cash like beads at a Mardi Gras parade without requesting a receipt for backup, in other words, areas where you are, for the most part, having a ball living a carefree existence, thinking that you have the tiger firmly by the tail.

> **Adam was human; he didn't want the apple for the apple's sake; he wanted it because it was forbidden.**
>
> *Mark Twain*

It may sound silly to most of you, but people by nature spend money for no other reason than to simply spend it for the sake of spending it, utilize it for its intended purpose, throw it to the winds. There's more of it at the bank . . . What? Plow my extra green bucks into some savings account black hole?

These natural people find themselves at the end of each month looking in the mirror, scratching their head and asking, "WHERE DID MY MONEY GO?"

Examining your cash flow, which includes calculating your income, expenses, and savings, will give you a snapshot of where you truly are today so that you can clearly understand what it will take for you to get to a financially secure tomorrow. This part of the waste line exercise will begin to show you the importance of discipline and careful measurement of each and every dollar that enters and leaves your wallet or purse for the remainder of your life.

GATHERING RECEIPTS

─────────────────┤ Do This Now ├─────────────────

The two things that most of you will need at this point to track your cash flow will be your checking account ledger and available cash receipts. Now is the time to haul them out for reference.

The money that enters your wallet or checking account will be easy to identify and record by also having on hand all household wage and salary stubs as well as all statements that reflect dividends, interest, annuities, pensions, social security, tips, commissions, and any other form of recorded income.

Investment income from IRAs, 401(k)s and other retirement plans should *not* be included because these amounts are not available to you until you retire.

Monitoring your cash flow at home will be akin to monitoring your exercise routine at the health club. Just as you account for the number of dollars spent on various items throughout any given day, your exercise routine requires you to account for the number of burned calories, repetitions, and pounds of weight lifted throughout any given routine.

THE OBJECTIVE FOR EACH EXERCISE IS TO INCREASE YOUR STRENGTH: The physical exercise will increase your muscle mass, while this financial exercise will increase your money mass.

The accumulation of cash receipts will be the tricky part because it will force you to pay close attention to where your money goes (expenses), to ask the clerk at the convenience store for a receipt for your coffee and newspaper, to take a moment out (while the next customer pushes you along) to tuck the receipt into a prearranged spot in your wallet or purse, and then of course to add all specific receipts according to the selected category and record the figure on the Cash Flow Worksheet.

Chuck, Linda, and Michael had not maintained cash receipts prior to their introduction to *Wealth Workout*—let's face it, most of us don't—so they had to estimate much of their discretionary cash expenses used for things such as vacations, restaurants, entertainment, gas, coffee, newspapers, lunches, soft drinks, and other miscellaneous grocery items.

Each family calculated their annual expenses to arrive at an average monthly figure. THE OBJECTIVE OF THIS CASH FLOW EXERCISE IS TO FIND OUT HOW MUCH CAME IN AND WHERE IT WENT OUT.

Each family used their prior year tax return and wage statement stubs to calculate the amount spent on taxes. They also went back and looked at prior-year checking account ledgers and credit card statements to figure out what they had spent in each category. Credit cards were typically used for clothing, entertainment, restaurants, vacations, and gifts.

Chuck, Linda, and Michael could not believe over the course of one year how much more quickly their cash flowed out than flowed in. They were in shock! You may be surprised as well when you finish this workout.

If you are married, be certain to include all spousal accounts if maintained separately. Additional required materials will also be self-evident by examining the cash flow itemized list. As you gather this documentation from various nooks and crannies of your humble abode, it would be wise of you to CREATE SEPARATE FILES for existing and future statements and receipts for each category of savings, income, and expense. You can purchase a 50-count box of legal size manila files at any office supply store.

—————————————| Do This Now |—————————————

Once you have completed the task over this coming week of compiling your receipts and statements while creating files for each specific subcategory (i.e., mortgage payments, credit cards, medical), use your handy calculator (if necessary) and add all figures for one full month *and* for the entire year.

YOUR INCOME LESS YOUR EXPENSES EQUALS YOUR CASH FLOW. If your end result is positive, you have discovered some previously unaccounted for cash (income). If your result is a negative, look forward to a positive turnaround in Weeks Four and Five.

One final word about compiling your cash receipts: If you have only been able to gather receipts for the past week in areas such as "restaurants," rather than estimate expenses, simply total up the weekly figure and multiply by four to give you a monthly total. "Gee," you may be saying to yourself at this moment, "on one hand they want me gather specific expense receipts, but on the other hand they are asking me to extrapolate a week's worth of those receipts to arrive at a monthly total. How accurate of a picture will that be?"

Don't push it; we are attempting to keep this exercise as PAIN-LESS AND SIMPLE as possible for you while also attempting to straighten out your financial life.

Let's face it, all of us are creatures of habit. If you have had a tendency over the past few wage-earning years to dine out three to four times a week, we feel that it is safe to assume (and extrapolate) that you dine out at least 12 times per month. So don't get too hung up with the methodology here; do not lose your zest for enthusiastic participation! You have to get a feel for where you spend your discretionary cash. It will not be exact, but it will be telling.

As you move forward through the *Wealth Workout* program, you will acquire the habit of tracking nearly every penny that slips through your fingers while gaining a sense of pride that you are finally taking control of your financial future.

RECORDKEEPING

Before we move too far away from our discussion of creating records and getting organized, we promised to share with you some helpful tips on record keeping.

For starters, do not get down on yourself or take your disorganization as a personal affront to your self-worth; most Americans are totally disorganized.

We are bombarded each day with so much information in the form of paperwork, coupled with enormous time constraints, it's no wonder that organization has become a cottage industry in America; people just like yourself go out and actually hire a professional organizer to come into their home to keep their records organized!

Actually, a bit of the pack rat mentality exemplified by Pat and Ruth would be good for anybody's record-keeping system. You never know when those piles of paper will come to the rescue in an IRS tax audit or perhaps prove the value of the cellular telephone stolen from your vehicle.

THE KEY TO ANY RECORD KEEPING SYSTEM IS TO KEEP IT FUNCTIONAL. Throw out the shoe boxes and pick up a couple of used two-or four-drawer file cabinets. You will always find them for sale in your local newspaper classifieds, usually under "office supplies/furniture."

What to Keep:

- Keep separate files for each applicable category listed on your Cash Flow and Net Worth Worksheets.

- Keep all cash receipts. Each time you spend a discretionary penny, politely ask for a receipt to tuck away, and when you arrive home write down on your monthly ledger the nature of your purchase and the amount paid.

- Keep all key real estate documents in separate files by property name in order to avoid the confusion of sorting out specific deeds, contracts, promissory notes, or title policies.

- Keep separate files for canceled checks, monthly bank statements, and credit card accounts.

- Keep all annual mutual fund statements, trade confirmations, and dividend-reinvestment statements in separate files according to the name of the fund.

- Keep all annual IRA, 401(k), and other retirement plan statements.

- Keep all income tax returns and related documents that support all income and deductions for each yearly return.

- Keep records pertaining to the sale of all stocks, mutual funds, and other investments or assets for a period of at least six years.

IT IS IMPORTANT TO MAINTAIN A MONTHLY LEDGER, a sort-of "draft" cash flow statement. Throughout each month, record all money earned and all money burned on a daily basis. At the end of each month, tally up each category and record it on a clean copy of your cash flow statement.

Another way to polish up on your record-keeping skills is to go high-tech, provided you are one of the growing number of Americans who are becoming PC literate.

You can effectively use your personal computer to pay bills, track balances in your bank and investment accounts, code your expenses for ease of accountability at tax time, and review fancy colored pie charts to show you where your money is going. Popular software programs for this purpose abound and can be purchased at any store that sells computers and peripheral equipment.

However, keep in mind that technology does not relieve you of the responsibility of maintaining hard copy records. For now you can't escape the world of paper, so hunker down for the next 76 days and grab the classifieds. You have some filing cabinets to buy!

SELECTING A PERSONAL MONEY TRAINER

Radical changes in lifestyle, no matter the change, often require professional help. And so it goes with your money; any radical changes in the flow of your hard-earned dollars will trip a variety of confusing bells and whistles.

As we touched on earlier, you may be a candidate for a personal money trainer, a professional confidant that can help you make sense of your own personal plan on Main Street as well as interpret for you the often conflicting news from Wall Street.

SO WHO DO YOU SELECT AS YOUR PERSONAL MONEY TRAINER? That's a very good question and one that is on the lips of more and more Americans. For years, Americans pretty much ignored financial matters, leaving issues of high finance to high rollers. Not so today.

Activity on Wall Street is mentioned in every television and radio newscast, mailboxes are stuffed to the gills with personal finance magazines, and the hottest mutual fund play is becoming ordinary small talk over lunch at the office or over league bowling games. There is an avalanche of financial information being crammed down the throat of the American consumer with very few commonsense explanations.

Before you can answer the above question on *who* to select as your personal money trainer, you need to have some basic background on *how* to go about finding the right one.

A number of planners, brokers, accountants, and insurance agents call themselves "financial advisors." Some have advanced educational credentials, and some do not. Your personal money trainer should have advanced education and training.

The following designations and credentials will help you understand who you are talking to in terms of sizing up experience:

- **(CPA) Certified Public Accountant.** An accountant who has passed a grueling state-administered examination that focuses on accounting practices and tax issues. Many CPAs today have also educated themselves on the subjects of investments and financial planning in order to offer their tax and accounting clients a one-stop approach to handling their financial future.

- **(EA) Enrolled Agent.** A tax preparer who has passed a difficult two-day tax exam administered by the IRS, which allows her or him to represent clients before the IRS. Many EAs are educating themselves on the subject of investments and financial planning in order to offer their tax clients one-stop tax and financial services.

- **(CFP) Certified Financial Planner.** A financial planner who has passed exams accredited by the Certified Financial Planner Board of Standards, a regulatory body that sets CFP standards. The tests focus on an applicant's ability to coordinate a client's estate, insurance, investments, and tax affairs.

- **(ChFC) Chartered Financial Consultant.** A designation awarded by The American College to financial planners who complete 10 courses and 20 hours of examinations covering economics, insurance, taxation, estate planning and other related areas. They must also have at least three years of experience in the field of finance.

- **(CFA) Chartered Financial Analyst.** This designation concentrates on portfolio management and securities analysis. It is awarded by the Institute of Chartered Financial Analysts to financial analysts and others who pass exams in economics, financial accounting, portfolio management, securities analysis, and standards of conduct.

- **Registered investment advisor.** Someone who has registered with the Securities and Exchange Commission to give financial advice to clients for a fee. All individuals who offer financial advice for a fee must be registered as an investment advisor or investment advisor agent.

- **Registered representative.** A stockbroker or account executive with a brokerage firm. To be registered, a broker must pass one or more licensing exams administered by the National Association of Securities Dealers. All individuals who sell securities for a commission must be registered.

The effort necessary to earn the above designations and registrations is an indication of an individual's level of commitment to the profession. However, there is more to know than a designation.

Given most Americans' busy schedules and lack of time and training in the financial arena, an ideal financial advisor will have expertise in all areas of financial planning. This should include taxes, budgeting and cash flow, financial statements, investments, insurance, college funding, and retirement/estate planning. It should be someone who understands all aspects of your financial situation and who can make recommendations based on your whole financial situation not just one specific area.

An ample dose of trust is always a healthy ingredient to add to your selection recipe. After all, we are talking about your hard-earned dollars.

It is also advisable to clearly understand how your personal money trainer expects to be compensated for his or her services.

Finacial Planners are Compensated in Three Distinct Ways:

1. **Hourly fee.**   Planners who charge an hourly fee generally do not give specific product advice. Pro: They are technically strong and can produce a plan. Con: They only do half the job. You still have to find someone to recommend the products to implement your plan, and you will pay for that advice: Result: You pay twice unless you are willing to do it yourself.

2. **Fee based on assets under management.**   Planners compensated in this way typically provide you with a plan and recommend specific investments. They are paid an annual fee up to 3 percent of the assets they manage on your behalf. Pro: They provide you with both the plan and the implementation. They give you confidence in their objectivity because they are not receiving a commission based on picking a specific product. They must provide you with ongoing support and service to earn their fees. If they don't, you fire them. Make sure your personal money trainer provides the services we discuss over the next few pages.

3. **Commission.**   Planners receive a commission on products they recommend. Many very good planners are compensated by commissions. Pro: They provide you with a plan and recommend the products to implement your plan. Con: They could sell you the wrong product at the wrong time in order to receive a commission, and they may not provide you with all the services described below.

Of course, you can always avoid the compensation issue altogether by taking the "do-it-yourself" route to planning and investment product selection and purchasing no-load funds.

It was recently reported that about 45 percent of all mutual fund dollars invested over the past couple of years were plowed into no-load funds.

If you have ever watched the value of your no-load fund go south, you may be saying to yourself that you bought the wrong thing at the wrong time for the wrong reason. This is not to suggest that no-load funds are bad, but when the market begins to wreak havoc, WHO DO YOU TURN TO FOR ANSWERS?

An excellent example that illustrates this dilemma was recently told by Nick Murray, a popular financial services author. Americans think that when their utility fund is down 20 percent, they'd better sell because somehow utilities are going "down the tubes." So they go in the den, turn on the *electric* light, run a pencil through the *electric* pencil sharpener, and write their redemption request. Then they go downstairs, turn on the *electric* light in the kitchen, take a frozen pizza out of the *electric* refrigerator, pop it in the *electric* microwave, and turn on the *electric* TV to watch "Gloom and Doom Today."

You have also probably learned that the customer service representative at the no-load fund's 800 number isn't exactly explaining things to your satisfaction.

The point here is that your personal money trainer will offer you the one thing a no-load fund buyer doesn't get: HELP—good, caring, professional help.

A well-educated, trusted professional will provide you with the following services to earn his or her fee or commission.

• An understanding of your tax situation.

- Assist in developing a comprehensive plan or a specific plan directed at a specific issue such as retirement or college funding.
- Assist you in "quantifying" your financial goals.
- Pointing out your options and alternatives to accomplish your financial goals.
- Evaluating your current investment and insurance policies.
- Providing you with strategies to cut expenses and taxes.
- Researching investment products and strategies.
- Researching insurance products and strategies.
- Presenting you with investment and insurance options to meet your needs and achieve your goals.
- Preparing and processing paperwork.
- Resolving customer service problems.
- Monitoring your investments.
- Providing reports showing investment performance.
- Making recommendations to modify your strategies based on market conditions and/or changes in you life.
- Assistance in liquidations, redemptions, and exchanges.
- Providing you with an annual checkup.
- Answering your questions and concerns.
- Helping you implement your *Wealth Workout* program.

So now that you have a general understanding of the personal money trainer professional designations and registrations, how they earn their keep, and how they will add significant value to the development of your financial future, we have come full circle to our previous question: WHO DO YOU SELECT AS YOUR PERSONAL MONEY TRAINER?

Here are some concluding helpful tips:

- Begin your search with recommendations from people you TRUST, such as family, friends, colleagues, or an accountant. In fact, ask your tax preparer if he or she provides this advice.

- The person should not only be an effective speaker but, more importantly, a GOOD LISTENER—one who will attempt to understand your lifestyle with your best interests at heart.
- Aggressively inquire about their EDUCATION, CREDENTIALS, and EXPERIENCE.
- Before you conclude your interview, openly discuss COMPENSATION.
- Before you sign one up, pick up the telephone and be *certain* that he or she has a CLEAN RECORD; inquire about any disciplinary actions by calling the Securities and Exchange Commission (SEC) (800) 732-0330, and the National Association of Securities Dealers (NASD), (800) 289-9999.

CONGRATULATIONS!

To briefly recap, these are the major milestones you have passed thus far in the program:

You have identified your goals!

You have evaluated your current financial situation!

The next exercise in Week 3 will show you how much cash you will need to invest each month to achieve those goals.

One word of caution: Be prepared to alter your current spending habits.

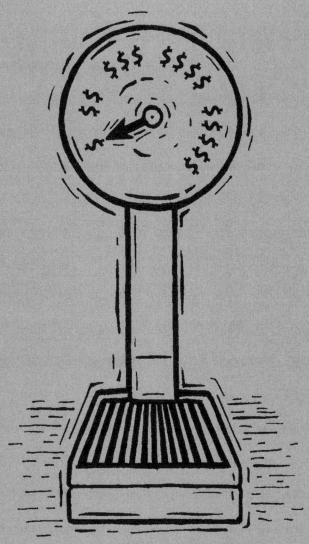

Week 3
YOUR PERSONAL FITNESS PLAN

YOUR PERSONAL FITNESS PLAN

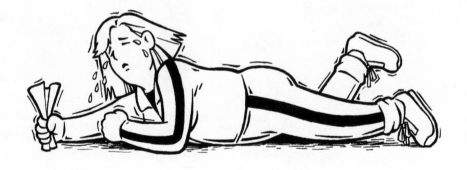

Week 3 Warm-Up Exercise:

1. Lie on your back with one arm behind your head.
2. With your free hand, gently grasp your Weeks 1 and 2 worksheets; slowly inhale; hold for a moment, examine the gap between where you are (net worth and cash flow) where you want to be (goals), and what it's going to take to get there (fitness plan).
3. Upon completion, roll over onto your stomach and have a good cry.

Personal Fitness Worksheet
as of _____

Goals, Priority, and Amount	Amounts Needed to Invest per Month		Number of	
	at 6%	at 10%	Months	Years
_____	_____	_____	____	____
_____	_____	_____	____	____
_____	_____	_____	____	____
_____	_____	_____	____	____
_____	_____	_____	____	____
_____	_____	_____	____	____
_____	_____	_____	____	____
_____	_____	_____	____	____
_____	_____	_____	____	____
_____	_____	_____	____	____
Total	_____	_____	____	____

Think how wonderful it will feel for you to be living and experiencing one of your goals made possible because of your commitment, purpose, and plan. THIS IS THE WEEK YOU BEGIN TO CREATE YOUR PERSONALIZED PLAN FOR ACHIEVING FINANCIAL FITNESS.

> **Great minds have purposes, others have wishes.**
>
> *Washington Irving*

It has been said that plans are funny things: Without them, we seldom reach our goals. The beauty of planning is that the process is quite simple, but the choices made along the way may prove at times to be a little difficult.

For the next seven days, you will perform SIMPLE CALCULATIONS that will reveal how much money you must invest on a monthly basis to realize the goals that you thoughtfully selected during Week 1.

This financial fitness plan workout is centered around factors that similarly affect a physical fitness or weight-reduction plan, namely, that it provides you with a framework and some balance.

For example, let's assume you've started a routine at the health club with a goal to tone up the pecks and tighten the butt. You have worked out a plan with the help of a personal trainer who helps you to decide on the type of exercise, the number of repetitions, and the number of sets necessary to reach your goal. The problem is that you, like most Americans, want results today, want to have that rock-hard butt and bulging set of pecks overnight.

You figure that your goal will be reached at the speed of light if you work out seven days a week, 10 hours a day. This would be unrealistic for most of us, unless of course you decide your goal is to end up in the emergency room at St. Vincent's Hospital. A realistic alternative to balance out your life and achieve the same goal would be to work out three days a week for one hour a day. You will eventually acquire the desired sculptured look; it will simply take a longer period of time.

A weight-reduction plan also calls for balance in order to successfully achieve a healthy, comfortable lifestyle. For example, you have just given yourself a good look-over in front of the mirror at home and have told yourself you will either lose some big-time weight or run away with the circus. Quickly remembering your phobia of lions and tigers and bears, you decide to be serious about dropping the extra flab.

One sure-fired way to lose the goo is to starve yourself by living on bread and water for six weeks. This of course is unrealistic, considering your penchant for pot pies and tutti-frutti ice cream. A realistic alternative to balance out your life and achieve the same goal would be to reduce your caloric and fat intake, thereby gradually losing weight without killing yourself. You will eventually arrive at your desired weight; it will simply take a longer period of time.

As previously mentioned, THE FINANCIAL FITNESS PLAN THAT YOU BEGIN TO CREATE THIS WEEK WILL PROVIDE YOU WITH THE FRAMEWORK FOR PROJECTING HOW MUCH MONEY IT'S GOING TO TAKE TO ACHIEVE YOUR GOALS. Throughout this process, you may think that your annual income or other obstacles will prevent you from achieving your goals. We encourage you to keep an open and positive mind. Remember, you are only at the beginning phase of the planning process.

After you successfully complete this week's exercise of examining how much money it will take, the following two weeks of CUTTING THE FAT will show you *exactly* how you will arrive at each financial goal!

It will probably require some trade-offs in terms of your time horizon to realize a goal and perhaps some modification in terms of prioritizing your goal achievements. But the point is this: YOU CAN AND WILL REALIZE YOUR FINANCIAL GOALS.

The amount of money you must save and invest to realize each and every financial goal depends a great deal upon the following two factors:

1. Your commitment to change or adjust your lifestyle, which we will cover at length in Weeks 4 and 5.
2. How and where you invest your excess cash.

UNDERSTANDING RATE OF RETURN

Investing your excess cash will be explored throughout the remainder of this book, but for purposes of understanding how you will acquire, over time, the necessary cash to realize your financial goals, IT IS IMPORTANT FOR YOU TO UNDERSTAND THE RATE OF RETURN ON YOUR INVESTMENT.

Rate of return provides the same thing for your dollar as carbohydrates provide for your diet—a specific level of energy for the desired level of productivity. One way to illustrate the rate of return is by examining Table 3–1.

TABLE 3–1:   Growth of Annual Investment of $1,000
(Invested at the Beginning of Each Year)

Years Invested	Percentage Rate of Return				
	4%	6%	8%	10%	12%
1	$1,040	$1,060	$1,080	$1,100	$1,120
5	5,600	6,000	6,300	6,700	7,100
10	12,500	14,000	15,600	17,500	19,700
15	20,800	24,700	29,300	35,000	41,800
20	31,000	39,000	49,400	63,000	80,700
25	43,300	58,200	79,000	108,200	149,300

Source: H.D. Vest Financial Services

The message here is threefold:

1. There is an extraordinary difference in the amount of money you can accumulate with seemingly small differences in the annual percentage rate of return.
2. The link between time and rate of return is a powerful combination.
3. It is important to begin to build your asset base today rather than postponing your investment until tomorrow.

The overwhelming reason to begin this *Wealth Workout* program today is to secure your finances for tomorrow: THERE ARE NO QUICK FIXES THAT PRODUCE LONG-TERM RESULTS. The longer your money is invested, the more it will produce once you put together your systematic investment plan.

For example, let's assume your investment dollars are earning a 10 percent compounded annual rate of return. If you are investing

$100 per month starting at the age of 30, your systematic plan will generate $379,664 by the time you reach the age of 65. Beginning with the same rate of return and monthly amount at the age of 40 will generate $132,683, a more modest amount but certainly not chicken feed.

WHEN THE RETURNS FROM SYSTEMATIC INVESTING ARE SO SUBSTANTIAL, WHY DO SO MANY AMERICANS DO NOTHING TO BUILD WEALTH? Our friend Chuck had a number of reasons (i.e., excuses) for not having an investment plan, none greater than his lack of focus on the future; he simply had no specific financial goals. Although he did manage to tuck away a minimal amount each year, Chuck did not have a systematic investment plan of any consequence. Michael and Linda were too busy keeping up with the Joneses to give an investment plan a moment of thought. Each of them felt a gnawing in their gut that "something" was wrong with their financial picture, but neither of them were willing to take the time to discuss the basis for their feelings. This was very strange considering that Michael was a bankruptcy consultant.

Pat and Ruth had the most on the ball in terms of finding a way to systematically stash their hard-earned cash for retirement, despite the overwhelming financial drain of raising three children. Yes, they were committed to a savings plan, but unfortunately it was only that, a savings plan, rather than an investment program. Their nest egg could be *significantly* larger today if they had invested for a higher rate of return than was being offered with a CD through their local bank.

To help you get started with this exercise, we will show you the process that Chuck, Linda and Michael, and Pat and Ruth worked through to determine how much money they needed to accumulate in order to achieve their personal financial goals.

––––––––––––––––––––––⊣ **Do This Now** ⊢––––––––––––––––––––––

If you have not already done so, now would be a good time to transfer your list of goals from your Week 1 Financial Goals Worksheet to your Week 3 Personal Fitness Worksheet found at the beginning of this exercise.

Below, you will see how our households completed their worksheets. Don't be intimidated with the calculations. In the remainder of this chapter, we will walk you through a series of easy steps to complete your worksheet.

Chuck

| | Amounts Needed to Invest per Month (Rate of Return) | | Number of | |
Goals	at 6%	at 10%	Months	Years
Emergency fund $15,000	$ 314 (a)	$ 314 (a)	36	3
New furniture $10,000	254	239	36	3
New car $10,000	143	129	60	5
Condo down payment $15,000	92	73	120	10
Retirement $1,137,000	667	247	360	30
Total	$ 1,470	$ 1,003		

(a) Earning a 4% rate of return.

Chuck's Conclusion: In order to achieve his specific goals, he must invest $1,470 per month earning a 6 percent rate of return or $1,003 per month earning a 10 percent rate of return for "x" number of months (except for his emergency fund, which would earn a 4 percent rate of return). A little belt-tightening, but it's doable.

Michael and Linda

| | Amounts Needed to Invest per Month (Rate of Return) | | Number of | |
Goals	at 6%	at 10%	Months	Years
Pay credit cards $10,000	$ 499 (a)	$ 499 (a)	24	2
Emergency fund $36,000	528 (b)	528 (b)	60	5

Goals	at 6%	at 10%	Months	Years
College fund (Eric) $47,300	1,271	1,197	36	3
College fund (Brad) $50,100	924	851	48	4
Buy cars $20,000	287	258	60	5
Buy boat $85,000	488	391	120	10
Retirement $2,493,000	2,497	1,147	300	25
Total	$ 6,494	$ 4,871		

(a) This money would be paid monthly to reduce credit card balances and would not earn a 6% or 10% rate of return.

(b) Earning a 4% rate of return.

Michael and Linda's Conclusion: Throw in the towel. (Just kidding) In order for them to achieve their lofty goals, they must invest $6,494 dollars per month earning a 6 percent rate of return or $4,871 dollars per month earning a 10 percent rate of return for "x" number of months (except for the credit payments and emergency fund as footnoted above). Looks like mac and cheese for a while.

Pat and Ruth

Goals	Amounts Needed to Invest per Month (Rate of Return)		Number of	
	at 6%	at 10%	Months	Years
Elder care $ 50,000	$ 0	$ 0		
New car $ 15,000	0	0		
Vacation home $ 80,000	0	0		
Retirement $1,263,000	2,120	1,180	180	15
Total	$ 2,120	$ 1,180		

Pat and Ruth's Conclusion: If you recall from Week 2, Pat and Ruth had accumulated $150,000 to realize three of their four goals; therefore, zeros were put on their worksheet because no additional funds needed to be invested for the first three goals. They also had sufficient cash for an emergency fund. However, in order for them to realize their goal of a secure retirement, they will need to invest $2,120 dollars per month earning a 6 percent rate of return or $1,180 dollars per month earning a 10 percent rate of return for 180 months. No problem for this thrifty couple.

ELIMINATING DEBT

If you've been dreading trips to the mailbox recently for fear of the monster credit card bills that lurk within, Michael and Linda shared the same fear.

They were liberated from the addictive lure of free air miles and toasters, from the black hole of plastic, by using Table 3–2 to arrive at a monthly payment amount. Their goal was to pay off their credit card balances of $10,000 over 24 months. Refer to Table 3–2 and you will see that they must pay $499 per month for the next 24 months to eliminate this debt. They must also refrain from using these cards in the future (which they have been doing).

⊢ Do This Now ⊢

	Linda and Michael	You
Enter your credit card balance:	$ 10,000	$ _____
Number of months to eliminate:	24	_____
Monthly payment per Table 3–2:	$ 499	$ _____

RECORD THE FIGURE ON YOUR PERSONAL FITNESS WORKSHEET.

CREATING AN EMERGENCY FUND

As we pointed out in Week 1, you need at least six months of net take-home pay for a reliable emergency fund. This provides

TABLE 3-2: Paying Off Your Credit Card Balances

Number of Months to Eliminate	Credit Card Balance					
	$2,000	$4,000	$6,000	$8,000	$10,000	$12,000
2	1,023	2,045	3,068	4,090	5,113	6,135
4	519	1,038	1,557	2,076	2,594	3,113
6	351	702	1,053	1,404	1,755	2,106
8	267	534	802	1,069	1,336	1,603
10	217	434	651	867	1,084	1,301
12	183	367	550	733	917	1,100
14	159	319	478	638	797	957
16	142	283	425	566	708	849
18	128	255	383	510	638	766
20	116	233	349	466	582	699
22	107	215	322	430	537	644
24	100	200	300	399	499	599

Assuming 18 percent interest charged by the credit card company.
Source: H.D. Vest Financial Services

ready access to cash to pay your day-to-day living expenses should you lose your job or face a financial crisis due to illness or accident.

After taking into account current liquid assets from the Net Worth Worksheet, Table 3–3 reveals that Chuck needed to invest $314 per month for three years and Linda and Michael needed to invest $528 per month for five years to build an adequate emergency fund.

───────────────────────── ┤ Do This Now ├─────────────────────────

Use the following table to calculate what it will take for you to build your emergency fund:

	Chuck	Linda and Michael	You
Current liquid assets from Net Worth Worksheet	$ 3,000	$ 1,000	$_____
Amount needed— from Goals Worksheet	15,000	36,000	_____
Shortfall =	(12,000)	(35,000)	
Months to save— from Goals Worksheet	36	60	_____
Monthly savings from Table 3–3	$ 314	$ 528	

MAKING LARGE PURCHASES

PROTECT YOURSELF . . . two words to the wise when considering a large purchase such as a new car, new furniture, a new bass boat, or perhaps a creek-side chalet that leads to a spring-fed pond.

You will either pay cash or arrange financing. Under either scenario, you will be required to sock some money away on a monthly basis to enjoy the purchase. Tables 3–4 and 3–5 reflecting cash and Table 3–6 reflecting a finance arrangement will help you determine the monthly amount that you will either have to pay or save to make your purchase.

Chuck wanted to save monthly to purchase furniture and a new car in lieu of financing. Linda and Michael also wanted to save monthly to buy cars and their boat. Pat and Ruth had sufficient savings to buy the new car they would need in three years and the vacation home they wanted to buy in five years.

As we progress through each workout, we will learn if their objectives were possible given each of their financial situations.

Chuck's Goals

	Furniture	New Car
Amount	$10,000	$10,000
Years to save	3	5
Monthly amount to save:		
Table 3–4 at 6%	$254	$143
Table 3–5 at 10%	$240	$129

TABLE 3-3: Calculating Monthly Savings for Emergency Fund

Time to Save (months)	Emergency Fund										
	$6,000	$8,000	$10,000	$12,000	$15,000	$20,000	$25,000	$30,000	$35,000	$40,000	$50,000
6	992	1,322	1,653	1,983	2,479	3,306	4,132	4,958	5,785	6,611	8,264
12	491	655	818	982	1,227	1,636	2,045	2,454	2,864	3273	4,091
24	241	321	401	481	601	802	1,002	1,203	1,403	1,604	2,005
36	157	210	262	314	393	524	655	786	917	1,048	1,310
48	115	154	192	231	289	385	481	577	674	770	962
60	90	121	151	181	226	302	377	452	528	603	754

Assuming 4 percent rate of return with interest reinvested.
Source: H.D. Vest Financial Services

Chuck's Conclusion: If he were to earn 6 percent on his savings, he would need to squirrel away $254 dollars per month for his furniture and $143 per month for his car.

On the other hand, if he *invested* his cash and earned 10 percent, he would only need $240 per month for the furniture and $129 for the car. It may be unrealistic for Chuck to earn a 10 percent return on money invested for his three-year goal to buy furniture. We will show you historical rates of returns on various investment options in Weeks 6 and 7, Pump It Up.

Linda and Michael's Goals

	Two Cars	Sailboat
Amount	$20,000	$80,000
Years to save	5	10
Monthly amount to save:		
Table 3–4 at 6%	$287	$488
Table 3–5 at 10%	$258	$391

Linda and Michael's Conclusion: Scratch the finance charges and build the necessary funds with cash. Sure, they could have driven their Mercedes and sailed the free wind much sooner, but take a look at Table 3–6, "Financing Large Purchases." They would have made monthly payments on the cars of $425 dollars for 5 years and for the boat, $1,057 for 10 years.

⊢ Do This Now ⊢

Your goals:	_____	_____
Amount	$ _____	$ _____
Years to save	_____	_____
Monthly amount to save:		
Table 3–4 at 6%	$ _____	$ _____
Table 3–5 at 10%	$ _____	$ _____

RECORD THE FIGURE ON YOUR PERSONAL FITNESS WORKSHEET.

TABLE 3–4: **Monthly Investments for Large Purchases Earning a 6%**
Rate of Return with Interest and Dividends Reinvested

Dollar Amount Needed for Purchase

Number of Years to Invest	$5,000	$10,000	$15,000	$20,000	$35,000	$50,000	$65,000	$80,000	$100,000
1	405	811	1,216	1,621	2,837	4,053	5,269	6,485	8,107
2	197	393	590	786	1,376	1,966	2,556	3,146	3,932
3	127	254	381	508	890	1,271	1,652	2,034	2,542
4	92	185	277	370	647	924	1,202	1,479	1,849
5	72	143	215	287	502	717	932	1,147	1,433
10	31	61	92	122	214	305	397	488	610
15	17	34	52	69	120	172	224	275	344
20	11	22	32	43	76	108	141	173	216
25	7	14	22	29	51	72	94	115	144
30	5	10	15	20	35	50	65	80	100

Source: H.D. Vest Financial Services

TABLE 3–5: **Monthly Investments for Large Purchases**
Earning a 10% Rate of Return with Interest and Dividends Reinvested

Dollar Amount Needed for Purchase

Number of Years to Invest	$5,000	$10,000	$15,000	$20,000	$35,000	$50,000	$65,000	$80,000	$100,000
1	398	796	1,194	1,592	2,785	3,979	5,173	6,367	7,958
2	189	378	567	756	1,323	1,891	2,458	3,025	3,781
3	120	240	359	479	838	1,197	1,556	1,915	2,393
4	85	170	255	341	596	851	1,107	1,362	1,703
5	65	129	194	258	452	646	839	1,033	1,291
10	24	49	73	98	171	244	317	391	488
15	12	24	36	48	84	121	157	193	241
20	7	13	20	26	46	66	86	105	132
25	4	8	11	15	26	38	49	60	75
30	2	4	7	9	15	22	29	35	44

Source: H.D. Vest Financial Services

TABLE 3–6: Monthly Payment for Financing Large Purchases

Number of Years	\$5,000	\$10,000	\$15,000	\$20,000	\$35,000	\$50,000	\$65,000	\$80,000	\$100,000
1	440	880	1,319	1,758	3,077	4,396	5,715	7,033	8,792
2	231	461	692	923	1,615	2,307	2,999	3,692	4,614
3	161	323	484	645	1,129	1,613	2,097	2,581	3,227
4	127	254	380	507	888	1,268	1,649	2,029	2,536
5	106	212	319	425	744	1,062	1,381	1,700	2,125
10	66	132	198	264	463	661	859	1,057	1,322
15	54	107	161	215	376	537	698	860	1,075
20	48	97	145	193	338	483	627	772	965
25	45	91	136	182	318	454	591	727	909
30	44	88	132	176	307	439	570	702	878

Assuming 10 percent finance charge.
Source: H.D. Vest Financial Services

HOME PURCHASE

HOW MUCH HOUSE CAN YOU AFFORD?

It's not just the down payment and mortgage payment. You must also consider additional expenses of home ownership including property taxes, home insurance, home maintenance and repairs, utilities, lawn care, and sprinkler systems.

For Linda and Michael, these items added an additional $5,500 to their annual expenses, or about $450 per month, in addition to the mortgage payment of $1,000 per month.

Chuck wants to put 10 percent down to buy his condo, which he estimates will cost $100,000. He must also save enough for the closing costs, which will cost another 3–5 percent on average, or $3,000 to $5,000. Therefore, Chuck believes he needs to save approximately $15,000 to move in, assuming he can qualify for a $90,000 mortgage. As you may well imagine, the mortgage rate at the time of his purchase will have a significant impact on his monthly payment and ability to qualify for a mortgage.

For example, by referring to Table 3–7, you can easily see that a $100,000 mortgage at 5 percent will require a monthly payment of $537 per month, slightly less than what Chuck is paying now for his apartment at $550 per month. But if he has to pay a rate of 10 percent, his payment increases to $878 per month.

He should also consider the additional expenses he will incur, which could amount to $300 to $450 per month for taxes, insurance, maintenance, and repairs. Of course, he will also want to furnish his new home, and home furnishings add up fast!

For this workout, we are going to calculate what you will need to save given your goal in Week 1. You may have to revise that goal based on what you can afford to pay.

As a rule of thumb, your mortgage payments plus taxes and insurance should not exceed 28 percent of your gross income.

For Chuck, this would limit him to a payment of $875 per month ($37,500 income divided by 12 months x .28). Assuming insurance and taxes of $300 per month, his monthly mortgage payment would be limited to $575 ($875 less $300). Given his current salary, Chuck's goal would be difficult to attain today unless he were able to secure a manageable mortgage rate.

Another rule of thumb to keep in mind is that your total debt payments should not exceed 36 percent of your gross income.

Continuing our example of Chuck, we want to know the amount of money he needs to save on a monthly basis to make his down payment and closing costs.

He has 10 years to save, and each year he can update his plan. As he gets closer to his goal and further educates himself on the local market, home prices, and available financing, it may certainly be necessary for him to modify his estimates.

Our point is that Chuck is doing *something* to achieve his goal and therefore will very likely reach it.

He understands the power of time and compounding relative to the time frame established to gather the funds. Also, Chuck believes his income will continue to increase over this 10-year period, thereby making it more likely that he will qualify for the mortgage.

The following table will help you find a true "bottom line" in terms of calculating the necessary cash for your down payment and closing costs:

	Chuck	**You**
Purchase price	$ 100,000	_____
Down payment	10%	_____
Cash needed for down payment	$ 10,000	_____
Closing costs (3–5%)	5%	_____
Cash needed for closing costs	$ 5,000	_____
Total needed	$ 15,000	_____
Years to save	10	_____
Monthly amount to save:		
Table 3–8 at 6%	$ 92	_____
Table 3–9 at 10%	$ 73	_____

RECORD THE FIGURE ON YOUR PERSONAL FITNESS WORKSHEET.

By subtracting your estimated down payment and closing costs from the purchase price, you will calculate the remaining mortgage amount. Find the total amount on Table 3–7 and read down the column to the desired mortgage rate. This figure is your estimated monthly mortgage payment.

TABLE 3–7:   Monthly Mortgage Payment for 30-Year Fixed Mortgage

Mortgage Rate	**Mortgage Amount**						
	$50,000	$75,000	$100,000	$125,000	$150,000	$175,000	$200,000
5%	268	403	537	671	805	939	1,074
6%	300	450	600	749	899	1,049	1,199
7%	333	499	665	832	998	1,164	1,331
8%	367	550	734	917	1,101	1,284	1,468
9%	402	603	805	1,006	1,207	1,408	1,609
10%	439	658	878	1,097	1,316	1,536	1,755
11%	476	714	952	1,190	1,428	1,667	1,905
12%	514	771	1,029	1,286	1,543	1,800	2,057
13%	553	830	1,106	1,383	1,659	1,936	2,212
14%	592	889	1,185	1,481	1,777	2,074	2,370
15%	632	948	1,264	1,581	1,897	2,213	2,529

Source: H.D. Vest Financial Services

TABLE 3–8:   Monthly Investment for Home Down Payment

Dollar Amount of Down Payment and Closing Costs

Number of Years	$5,000	$10,000	$15,000	$20,000	$25,000	$50,000	$75,000	$100,000
1	405	811	1,216	1,621	2,027	4,053	6,080	8,107
2	197	393	590	786	983	1,966	2,949	3,932
3	127	254	381	508	636	1,271	1,907	2,542
4	92	185	277	370	462	924	1,386	1,849
5	72	143	215	287	358	717	1,075	1,433
10	31	61	92	122	153	305	458	610
15	17	34	52	69	86	172	258	344
20	11	22	33	43	54	108	162	216
25	7	14	22	29	36	72	108	144
30	5	10	15	20	25	50	75	100

Assuming a 6 percent rate of return with interest and dividends reinvested.

Source: H.D. Vest Financial Services

TABLE 3–9:   Monthly Investment for Home Down Payment

Dollar Amount of Down Payment and Closing Costs

Number of Years	$5,000	$10,000	$15,000	$20,000	$25,000	$50,000	$75,000	$100,000
1	398	796	1,194	1,592	1,990	3,979	5,969	7,958
2	189	378	567	756	945	1,891	2,836	3,781
3	120	239	359	479	598	1,197	1,795	2,393
4	85	170	255	341	426	851	1,277	1,703
5	65	129	194	258	323	646	969	1,291
10	24	49	73	98	122	244	366	488
15	12	24	36	48	60	121	181	241
20	7	13	20	26	33	66	99	132
25	4	8	11	15	19	38	57	75
30	2	4	7	9	11	22	33	44

Assuming a 10 percent rate of return with interest and dividends reinvested.

Source: H.D. Vest Financial Services

EDUCATIONAL FUNDING

THE KEY TO SUCCESSFULLY SAVING ENOUGH MONEY FOR FUTURE EDUCATIONAL GOALS IS TO BEGIN EARLY. College costs are increasing at a rate of 6–15 percent annually, far outpacing medical costs or the price of a new car. You have already estimated in Week 1 the anticipated costs to fund your child's college education. Tables 3–10 and 3–11 will help you calculate the amount of money you will need to save on a monthly basis.

Linda and Michael had to accumulate approximately $50,000 for each child. Eric had three years before he entered college, so they needed to be aggressive and start saving $1,271 per month. Brad, on the other hand, had four years of high school remaining before he entered college; therefore, they needed to start saving $924 per month (based on a 6 percent annual rate of return on their investments).

If they earn more than 6 percent, which may be unrealistic given the short time frame they have to save, they would sock away smaller monthly amounts, as revealed in Table 3–10.

──────────────────── ┤ **Do This Now** ├ ────────────────────

Referring to Tables 3–10 and 3–11, determine the monthly amount that you must invest based upon the cost of your selected college and years until your child's attendance.

RECORD THE FIGURE ON YOUR PERSONAL FITNESS WORKSHEET.

───

RETIREMENT FUNDING

Mention retirement and what springs to mind? Fishing? More golf? You wish. Try part-time work.

Today, people are living longer, healthier lives. This is wonderful provided they have the means to enjoy it. In Week 1, you calculated the total amount of money you will need to support at least 80 percent of your current standard of living in retirement.

Wealth Workout understands that you will work your whole life hoping to obtain some comfort, some security, to be able to spend

TABLE 3-10:   How Much to Invest Monthly to Pay Future
College/Educational Costs

Cost of College/Educational Program

Years to College	$50,000	$75,000	$100,000	$125,000	$150,000	$175,000	$200,000	$225,000
1	4,053	6,080	8,107	10,133	12,160	14,187	16,213	18,240
2	1,966	2,949	3,932	4,915	5,898	6,881	7,864	8,847
3	1,271	1,907	2,542	3,178	3,813	4,449	5,084	5,720
4	924	1,386	1,849	2,311	2,773	3,235	3,697	4,159
5	717	1,075	1,433	1,792	2,150	2,508	2,867	3,225
6	579	868	1,157	1,447	1,736	2,025	2,315	2,604
7	480	721	961	1,201	1,441	1,681	1,922	2,162
8	407	611	814	1,018	1,221	1,425	1,628	1,832
9	350	525	701	876	1,051	1,226	1,401	1,576
10	305	458	610	763	915	1,068	1,220	1,373
11	268	403	537	671	805	939	1,073	1,208
12	238	357	476	595	714	833	952	1,071
13	212	319	425	531	637	743	849	956
14	191	286	381	477	572	667	762	858
15	172	258	344	430	516	602	688	774
16	156	234	311	389	467	545	623	701
17	142	212	283	354	425	495	566	637
18	129	194	258	323	387	452	516	581

Assuming a 6 percent rate of return with interest and dividends reinvested.
Source: H.D. Vest Financial Services

a little less time thinking about money and more time spending it on your grandchildren. However, before we get ahead of ourselves, you must calculate what it's going to take for you to turn this goal of more leisure and less stress into reality.

According to the U.S. Department of Labor, 33 percent of your retirement income will come from personal assets.

TABLE 3–11: How Much to Invest Monthly to Pay Future College/Educational Costs

Cost of College/Educational Program

Years to College	$50,000	$75,000	$100,000	$125,000	$150,000	$175,000	$200,000	$225,000
1	3,979	5,969	7,958	9,948	11,937	13,927	15,917	17,906
2	1,891	2,836	3,781	4,726	5,672	6,617	7,562	8,508
3	1,197	1,795	2,393	2,992	3,590	4,188	4,787	5,385
4	851	1,277	1,703	2,129	2,554	2,980	3,406	3,832
5	646	969	1,291	1,614	1,937	2,260	2,583	2,906
6	510	764	1,019	1,274	1,529	1,784	2,039	2,293
7	413	620	827	1,033	1,240	1,447	1,654	1,860
8	342	513	684	855	1,026	1,197	1,368	1,539
9	287	431	575	718	862	1,005	1,149	1,293
10	244	366	488	610	732	854	976	1,098
11	209	314	419	523	628	733	837	942
12	181	271	362	452	543	633	723	814
13	157	236	315	393	472	550	629	708
14	137	206	275	344	412	481	550	618
15	121	181	241	302	362	422	483	543
16	106	159	213	266	319	372	425	478
17	94	141	188	235	282	329	376	423
18	83	125	167	208	250	291	333	375

Assuming a 10 percent rate of return with interest and dividends reinvested.
Source: H.D. Vest Financial Services

Sources of Retirement Income

#1 Source = Personal Assets

33% of Retirement Income

Source: U.S. Department of Health and Human Services, 1992.

That is why it is essential not only to plan but also to make sure you are GETTING THE MOST FOR YOUR RETIREMENT DOLLARS.

The following instructions will show you how to calculate what additional monthly savings will be required of you to reach your retirement Shangri-la:

──────────────────┤ **Do This Now** ├──────────────────

Determine your additional monthly savings for retirement by following these instructions:

1. First, enter 80 percent of your current annual income under the column heading "You."

2. Enter the future retirement income you will need (after considering an annual inflation rate of 3 percent) by referring to Table 3–12. Find the annual income you calculated in step one and match it to the years to retirement.

3. Enter your projected Social Security benefits based on the Projected Annual Social Security Benefits in Table 3–13. To obtain a statement of your estimated benefits, call your local Social Security office at 1-800-772-1213 and ask for the Request for Statement of Earnings card, form SSA-7004.

4. Enter your projected annual pension. Contact your human resources department to determine the estimated pension benefit available to you at retirement. (Exclude benefits received from your contributions to a 401(k), 403(b), IRA, or SEP. These should be included in the next step.)

5. Enter the dollar amount that your *current* retirement assets will provide by referring to Tables 3–14 and 3–15. First, looking back at your Net Worth Worksheet (Week 2), find your total investment assets that you have already earmarked for retirement. Table 3–14 will show your annual income amount if these assets earn a 6 percent rate of return. Table 3–15 will show your annual income amount if these assets earn a 10 percent rate of return.

6. Subtract Social Security benefits, pension benefits, and projected retirement income benefits from current retirement assets from Future Annual Income Needed. This is the shortfall you will need to reduce by means of investing additional money.

7. Go to Tables 3–16 and 3–17 to determine the amounts you must invest on a monthly basis to fund your retirement goal shortfall calculated in step six.

8. Looking back at your Cash Flow Worksheet (Week 2), subtract what you are currently investing/saving per month.

9. Subtract line 8 from line 7. This final figure is the amount of *additional* cash you will need to add monthly to your current investments to reach your desired retirement income at 6 percent and 10 percent rates of return.

	Chuck	Linda and Michael	Pat and Ruth	You
1. Annual income needed	$30,000	$ 80,000	$ 60,000	$ _____
2. Future income needed—from Table 3–12	74,000	169,000	94,000	_____
3. Social Security benefits—from Table 3–13	16,000	27,000	23,000	_____
4. Pension	0	0	12,000	_____
5. Projected annual income from current retirement assets—from				
Table 3–14 at 6%	4,000	6,000	0	_____
Table 3–15 at 10%	13,000	16,000	0	_____
6. Retirement income gap: (Line 2 less Lines 3–5)				
At 6%	54,000	136,000	59,000	_____
At 10%	45,000	126,000	59,000	_____
* (Rounded)	50,000	130,000	60,000	_____
7. Needed Savings per Month—from				
Table 3–16 at 6%	750	2,830	3,120	_____
Table 3–17 at 10%	330	1,480	2,180	_____

Less

8. Current savings   83   333   1,000   _____
   per month (from Cash
   Flow Worksheet)

9. Additional required
   savings per month
   (Line 7 less Line 8)

At 6%	667	2,497	2120	_____
At 10%	247	1,147	1,180	_____

RECORD THE FIGURES ON YOUR PERSONAL FITNESS WORKSHEET.

CONGRATULATIONS!

The exercises performed and examples reviewed over the past week should have demonstrated once again that there are NO QUICK FIXES THAT PRODUCE LONG-TERM RESULTS.

However, it should be equally evident that your financial returns from your long-term effort will be substantial!

Based upon the gradual development of your personal financial plan, you now have a very good idea of how much cash it will take to achieve your retirement goals.

The following two weeks will show you how to get there by CUTTING THE FAT. As we mentioned earlier, be prepared to make some trade-offs in your lifestyle, but in doing so, also BE PREPARED TO REALIZE YOUR FINANCIAL DREAMS!

TABLE 3–12: Future Annual Income Needed at Retirement

Years to Retirement	Current Income								
	$ 20,000	$ 30,000	$ 40,000	$ 50,000	$ 60,000	$ 70,000	$ 80,000	$ 90,000	$ 100,000
45	$ 77,000	$ 116,000	$ 154,000	$ 193,000	$ 231,000	$ 270,000	$ 308,000	$ 347,000	$ 385,000
40	66,000	99,000	133,000	166,000	199,000	232,000	265,000	298,000	332,000
35	57,000	86,000	114,000	143,000	171,000	200,000	228,000	257,000	285,000
30	49,000	74,000	98,000	123,000	147,000	172,000	197,000	221,000	246,000
25	42,000	63,000	85,000	106,000	127,000	148,000	169,000	190,000	212,000
20	36,000	55,000	73,000	91,000	109,000	127,000	146,000	164,000	182,000
15	31,000	47,000	63,000	78,000	94,000	109,000	125,000	141,000	157,000
10	27,000	40,000	54,000	67,000	81,000	94,000	108,000	121,000	135,000
5	23,000	35,000	46,000	58,000	70,000	81,000	93,000	105,000	116,000

Assumes a 3% inflation rate.

TABLE 3–13: Projected Annual Social Security Benefits

Worker's Current Age		Worker's Earnings in 1991			
		$30,000	$40,000	$50,000	$55,000+
35	Worker	15,716	18,124	20,506	21,649
	Worker with Spouse	23,567	27,186	30,759	32,467
45	Worker	13,098	15,624	17,232	17,892
	Worker with Spouse	20,856	23,436	25,848	26,832
55	Worker	12,624	13,808	14,772	15,096
	Worker with Spouse	18,936	20,700	22,152	22,644
65	Worker	11,724	12,456	12,972	13,056
	Worker with Spouse	17,580	18,684	19,452	19,584

Source: Social Security Administration, 1992.

TABLE 3–14: Annual Income upon Retirement from Current Retirement Assets Earning a 6% Rate of Return

Years to Retirement	Current Retirement Assets								
	$ 5,000	$ 10,000	$ 20,000	$ 30,000	$40,000	$ 50,000	$ 60,000	$ 80,000	$ 100,000
45	$ 4,900	$ 9,800	$ 19,500	$ 29,300	$ 39,000	$ 48,800	$ 58,600	$ 78,100	$ 97,600
40	3,600	7,200	14,500	21,700	28,900	36,200	43,400	57,900	72,300
35	2,700	5,400	10,700	16,100	21,500	26,800	32,200	42,900	53,600
30	2,000	4,000	8,000	11,900	15,900	19,900	23,900	31,800	39,800
25	1,500	2,900	5,900	8,800	11,800	14,700	17,700	23,600	29,500
20	1,100	2,200	4,400	6,600	8,700	10,900	13,100	17,500	21,900
15	800	1,600	3,200	4,900	6,500	8,100	9,700	13,000	16,200
10	600	1,200	2,400	3,600	4,800	6,000	7,200	9,600	12,000
5	400	900	1,800	2,700	3,600	4,500	5,300	7,100	8,900

Assuming current retirement assets earn a rate of return of 6% before and after retirement at age 65, a 3% inflation rate and a life expectancy of 20 years after retirement.

TABLE 3–15: Annual Income upon Retirement from Current Retirement Assets Earning a 10% Rate of Return

	Current Retirement Assets								
Years to Retirement	$5,000	$10,000	$20,000	$30,000	$40,000	$50,000	$60,000	$80,000	$100,000
45	$29,200	$58,300	$116,700	$175,000	$233,400	$291,700	$350,000	$466,700	$583,400
40	17,700	35,500	70,900	106,400	141,800	177,300	212,700	283,700	354,600
35	10,800	21,600	43,100	64,700	86,200	107,800	129,300	172,400	215,500
30	6,500	13,100	26,200	39,300	52,400	65,500	78,600	104,800	131,000
25	4,000	8,000	15,900	23,900	31,800	39,800	47,800	63,700	79,600
20	2,400	4,800	9,700	14,500	19,400	24,200	29,000	38,700	48,400
15	1,500	2,900	5,900	8,800	11,800	14,700	17,600	23,500	29,400
10	900	1,800	3,600	5,400	7,100	8,900	10,700	14,300	17,900
5	500	1,100	2,200	3,300	4,300	5,400	6,500	8,700	10,900

Assuming current retirement assets earn a rate of return of 10% before retirement at age 65, a 6% rate of return after retirement, a 3% inflation rate, and a life expectancy of 20 years after retirement.

TABLE 3-16: Monthly Investment Required to Provide Retirement Funds

Retirement Income Needs

Years to Retirement	$30,000	$40,000	$50,000	$60,000	$70,000	$80,000	$90,000	$100,000	$110,000	$120,000	$130,000
45	$160	$220	$270	$330	$380	$440	$490	$550	$600	$660	$710
40	230	300	380	460	530	610	680	760	830	910	990
35	320	420	530	640	740	850	950	1,060	1,170	1,270	1,380
30	450	600	750	900	1,050	1,200	1,350	1,500	1,650	1,800	1,950
25	650	870	1,090	1,310	1,530	1,740	1,960	2,180	2,400	2,620	2,830
20	980	1,310	1,630	1,960	2,290	2,620	2,940	3,270	3,600	3,920	4,250
15	1,560	2,080	2,600	3,120	3,640	4,160	4,670	5,190	5,710	6,230	6,750
10	2,770	3,690	4,610	5,530	6,450	7,370	8,300	9,220	10,140	11,060	11,980
5	6,500	8,660	10,830	12,990	15,160	17,320	19,490	21,650	23,820	25,980	28,150

Assumes 6% rate of return earned before and after retirement at age 65, 3% inflation after retirement, and 20 years life expectancy after retirement.

TABLE 3–17: Monthly Investment Required to Provide Retirement Funds

Retirement Income Needs

Years to Retirement	$30,000	$40,000	$50,000	$60,000	$70,000	$80,000	$90,000	$100,000	$110,000	$120,000	$130,000
45	$40	$60	$70	$90	$100	$110	$130	$140	$160	$170	$190
40	70	100	120	140	170	190	210	240	260	290	310
35	120	160	200	240	280	320	360	400	440	480	520
30	200	270	330	400	470	530	600	670	730	800	870
25	340	450	570	680	790	910	1,020	1,130	1,250	1,360	1,480
20	590	790	990	1,190	1,390	1,590	1,780	1,980	2,180	2,380	2,580
15	1,090	1,450	1,820	2,180	2,540	2,910	3,270	3,630	4,000	4,360	4,720
10	2,210	2,940	3,680	4,410	5,150	5,880	6,620	7,350	8,090	8,820	9,560
5	5,830	7,780	9,720	11,670	13,610	15,550	17,500	19,490	21,390	23,330	25,280

Assumes 10% rate of return earned before and after retirement at age 65, 3% inflation after retirement, and 20 years life expectancy after retirement.

EXERCISE
four

Weeks 4 & 5
CUT THE FAT

CUT THE FAT

Weeks 4 and 5 Warm-Up Exercise:

1. While sitting up in a chair in slightly expectant fashion, firmly grasp your wallet, breath deeply and hold . . . slowly remove all discretionary cash.
2. While once again breathing normally, concentrate on your empty wallet.
3. Using all major muscle groups in your right or left hand, craft your personal expense reduction strategies on the worksheet areas below.

Cut the Fat Worksheet
as of _____

Expenses (from Cash Flow Worksheet)	Reduce by Monthly	Annually	Strategy
_____	_____	_____	_____
_____	_____	_____	_____
_____	_____	_____	_____
_____	_____	_____	_____
_____	_____	_____	_____
_____	_____	_____	_____
_____	_____	_____	_____
_____	_____	_____	_____
_____	_____	_____	_____

Total reductions _____ _____

COLD TURKEY TIME

The following two weeks of CUTTING THE FAT will put the seriousness of your efforts to the test, beginning with your Warm-up exercise of removing all discretionary cash and credit cards from your wallet or purse.

It is important for you to go cold turkey on this exercise for the next two weeks because your thought processes will be focusing on ways to reduce expenditures . . . the excess cash would be far too tempting for you to squander during such an emotionally vulnerable period of your life.

> **Poverty of course is no disgrace, but it is damned annoying.**
> *William Pitt*

--------| **Do This Now** |--------

Remove your cash, making a deposit to your checking account and remove all credit cards (save one for emergencies) . . . now, after you have calmed down from the shakes, let's move on to the all important strategies that will reshape your fiscal body. THE WHOLE POINT OF THIS EXERCISE IS FOR YOU TO GET A GRIP ON YOUR SPENDING AND BOOST YOUR EARNING POWER.

It is reported that Americans from coast to coast are taking a scissors to their spending, that a whopping three out of four say they trimmed their expenses in 1994, some by more than 10%.

Most admitted that they needed to take more CONTROL OVER THEIR FINANCIAL FUTURE.

HOW MUCH SNIPPING AND TRIMMING ARE YOU WILLING TO UNDERGO TO TAKE CONTROL OVER YOUR FUTURE?

In today's low-fat diet war between pretzels for breakfast and fat-free cookies for lunch, serious health nuts are maintaining a vigilant eye on product nutrition labels introduced in 1994 to keep a *daily* running tab of their fat intake.

"Fat content" is by far today's all-important physical health index for many Americans. In similar fashion, "expense content" is considered the all-important financial health index for all success-oriented Americans.

Therefore, if you can identify with the serious health enthusiasts that run a daily tab of their fat intake, this exercise is asking you to become a serious financial enthusiast by keeping a daily running tab of your expense intake. SO HOW DO YOU GET STARTED?

————————————┤ Do This Now ├————————————

To begin this exercise, transfer all of the "Your Expense" items (i.e., taxes, mortgage, etc.) applicable to your household from your Week 2 Cash Flow Worksheet to the vertical "Expense" column on your Cut the Fat Worksheet.

The remainder of this chapter will briefly discuss each item, offering various expense reduction strategies for your consideration. In addition to these, you may have specific strategies of your own.

Once you have decided on a strategy to reduce or eliminate a specific item from your expenses, enter on your Worksheet both monthly and annual figures. Also, make note of your strategy in the far right column.

At the end of the exercise, or the end of two weeks (whichever comes first), total all reductions and smile because you will have uncovered a significant amount of "missing money" that you will now be able to plow straight into your investments.

WE HAVE GIVEN YOU TWO WEEKS TO COMPLETE THIS EXERCISE because it involves an examination of more than 60 strategies to cut your expenses in a manner that calls upon you to focus on your *needs* versus your *wants*.

As a rule of thumb, approximately 70 percent of your monthly income is taken up by needs such as taxes, your mortgage or rent, car payments, and utilities.

Once these needs are met, the remaining 30 percent is reserved for the wants in your life, and IT IS HERE YOU MUST SERIOUSLY BEGIN TO ADJUST YOUR LIFESTYLE.

Do you need a new car, or can you survive by fixing your old one? You need to invest in more expensive clothing for work but what about the rest of the time?

HOW OUR SUCCESS STORIES CUT THE FAT

Let's first take a look at Chuck, Linda and Michael, and Pat and Ruth

1. Before they cut the fat.
2. After they cut the fat (90 days after the program).
3. TODAY (seven years later).

Incidentally, through the process of cutting the fat, all three households had three things in common:

1. All wished they had started sooner (don't we all . . .).
2. Regardless of goals or income, all were able to INCREASE THEIR SAVINGS RATE TO 20% !!!
3. They paid themselves first—20%—then paid their bills.

Chuck

	Before		After		7 Years Later	
Income	$ 37,500		$ 37,500		$ 54,000	
Taxes	(–) 10,400	(28%)	9,840	(26%)	15,700	(29%)
	(=) 27,100		27,660		38,300	
Expenses	(–) 26,100	(69%)	19,230	(52%)	27,500	(51%)
SAVINGS	$ 1,000	(3%)	$ 8,430	(22%)	$ 10,800	(20%)

Linda and Michael

	Before		After		7 Years Later	
Income	$ 100,000		$ 100,000		$ 150,000	
Taxes	(–) 32,150	(32%)	32,150	(32%)	45,000	(30%)
	(=) 67,850		67,850		105,000	
Expenses	(–) 62,650	(63%)	45,270	(45%)	75,000	(50%)
SAVINGS	$ 5,200	(5%)	$ 22,580	(23%)	$ 30,000	(20%)

Pat and Ruth

	Before		After		7 Years Later	
Income	$ 75,000		$ 75,000		$ 92,000	
Taxes	(–) 30,000	(40%)	26,850	(36%)	33,120	(36%)
	(=) 45,000		48,150		58,880	
Expenses	(–) 41,500	(55%)	31,600	(42%)	40,480	(44%)
SAVINGS	$ 3,500	(5%)	$ 16,550	(22%)	$ 18,400	(20%)

NOW, let's take a look at their CASH FLOW WORKSHEET EXPENSES in order for you to examine the practical strategies that each selected to CUT THE FAT. This will start the wheels to turn in your head when looking for ways to begin to CUT YOUR EXPENSE FAT.

We will then go on to suggest other strategies that you will want to consider using.

Chuck's Cut the Fat Worksheet

| | Reduction Amount | | | |
	Annual	Monthly	Yearly	Strategy
Fixed Expenses:				
Income taxes	$ 10,400	$ 47	$ 560	Open IRA
Mortgage or rent	6,600	0	0	
Utilities	600	5	60	Lower heat raise a/c
Telephone	600	5	60	Eliminate options
Total fixed	$ 18,200	$ 57	$ 680	
Variable Expenses:				
Food	$ 4,800	$ 100	$1,200	Use grocery list and budget
Medical	500	0	0	
Clothing	2,000	100	1,200	Watch for sales and budget
Auto insurance	850	0	0	
Auto maintenance	1,000	0	0	
Entertainment	2,000	50	600	Rent videos and budget
Restaurants	2,400	100	1,200	2 fewer dinners/month
Vacations	2,000	100	1,200	Package deals and budget
Gifts	2,000	100	1,200	Limit $ per person
Dry cleaning	600	0	0	
Total variable	$ 18,150	$ 550	$ 6,600	
Total expenses	$ 36,350	$ 607	$ 7,280	

Chuck's Fat-Reduction Analysis: In the previous workout, Chuck determined that he needed to invest $1,003 to $1,470 per month to achieve his goals. As you can see from the above worksheet, he was able to significantly increase his savings rate from 3 percent to 22 percent and reduce his spending by a whopping $607 dollars per month (or 20 percent!)

BUT, THE MOST IMPORTANT REVELATION FOR CHUCK WAS THAT HE BECAME KEENLY AWARE OF WHAT HE WAS SPENDING. The funny thing was that after the above expense reductions, he noticed no significant change in his lifestyle other than feeling deep in his heart that he had truly TAKEN CONTROL of his financial life.

He was not willing to give up much of his vacation or entertainment expense, considering that he remains single. However, he was continuing to do well at work, and his income continued to modestly increase each year by 5 percent over a period of 7 years. Therefore, he was allowed to continue to party while plowing most of his salary increases toward his original *Wealth Workout* goals.

Chuck reached his emergency fund goal over a period of four years rather than his original goal of three years and also purchased new leather furniture in 1992 after five years of plugging away the nickels rather than his original goal of three years.

Oh yes, in 1994 he also purchased his jet-black pre-owned import auto in first-class condition.

Chuck is currently investing monthly for his condo and retirement. Because his standard of living has increased and also because he now has less than 25 years to save for retirement, Chuck has increased his monthly retirement savings to $700 per month.

Also, because Chuck started saving late (not until 1992) for the down payment on his condo, he was left with only five years to accumulate his $15,000. Therefore, he more than doubled his monthly investment amount from $91 per month to $215 per month.

Chuck continues to save 20 percent of his income.

Michael and Linda's Cut the Fat Worksheet

	Reduction Amount			
	Annual	Monthly	Yearly	Strategy
Fixed Expenses:				
Taxes	$ 32,150	$ 0	$ 0	
Mortgage or rent	12,000	0	0	Sell home in 4 years
Utilities	1,600	33	400	Use candles & reduced a/c
Telephone	1,200	50	600	Cut long distance
Total fixed	$ 46,950	$ 83	$ 1,000	
Loan and debt payments:				
2 cars	$ 8,400	0	0	After leases, buy used
Variable Expenses:				
Food	$ 7,200	$ 100	$ 1,200	Use grocery list, coupons, join club
Medical	1,250	0	0	
Clothing	4,000	0	0	
Homeowner insurance	750	0	0	
Auto insurance	1,250	0	0	
Home maintenance	1,200	15	180	Cancel lawn service
Auto maintenance	2,000	0	0	
Entertainment	1,800	50	600	Scratch the movie, rent videos
Restaurants	2,600	100	1,200	1 dinner out per month
Vacations	6,600	500	6,000	Eliminate
Club memberships	600	50	600	Eliminate
Gifts	9,000	500	6,000	Specific amount per person
Dry cleaning	1,200	50	600	Only expensive silks
Total variable	$ 39,450	$ 1,365	$16,380	
Total expenses	$ 94,800	$ 1,448	$17,380	

Michael and Linda's Fat-Reduction Analysis: Linda and Michael desperately needed to eliminate from $4,871 to $6,494 dollars from their *monthly* expenses to achieve their goals . . . BIG BITES!

They could only find $1,448 per month (or 18 percent) to cut from their spending. This, however, allowed them to at least increase their savings rate from *4 percent to 23 percent!* Nonetheless, they knew that they had to make some *significant* changes in their lifestyle to achieve all of their goals.

The two flower-child refugees from the 1960s initially focused on reducing their credit card balances to zero by aggressively paying them off at the rate of $500 per month for two years. They also saved an additional $1,000 per month for their children's educational fund. They cut up their credit cards and scrupulously monitored their expenses on a *daily basis.*

Educational funding was a major concern. Scholarships were an option because both Eric and Brad were little Einsteins, and securing a loan remained a possibility. Of course, the kids would be expected to work part-time to fund some of the cost. But the uneasy question of how to secure adequate eductional funding loomed ever-greater on the scholastic horizon.

The following is the down and dirty of what happened to this frolicking family of the 80s: Eric was awarded a full engineering scholarship in 1990 (took after his father). That honor allowed sufficient savings for Brad to enter college in 1991. (Whew!) Brad also worked summers and part-time during school to support himself. In 1991, after both children flew the coop, Linda and Michael sold their three bedroom ranch-style home, freeing up $18,000 per year, or $1,500 per month in direct expenses. You guessed it, they went sassy and crazy, purchasing the sailboat of their dreams (financing and using equity from the home sale as a down payment), living on the boat for two years at the local marina.

Michael and Linda's income increased from $100,000 to $150,000 over a seven year period (7 percent per year). They were able and more than willing to pay off the boat loan in 18 months, moving back to solid ground by renting an apartment just in time for Christmas 1993. They were able to establish their emergency fund and were also able to save sufficient cash for the cars they would need to purchase when the two lease cars expired.

Their lease cars expired in late 1992 and early 1993. As each expired, Michael was able to replace each of them with a pre-owned Mercedes Benz, each in excellent condition and certified as such by their trustworthy "Dr. Benz." The cash outlay in 1992 was $4,000 and in 1993 was $10,000.

Michael and Linda were fast developing a practical side to themselves and decided that because each was entering his and her peak earning years, they would feel more comfortable with a fatter investment portfolio than with fatter tummies from devouring too many cheeseburgers in paradise somewhere in the Keys. Therefore, in 1994 they sold their sailing vessel for a profit and invested in a long-term project: a historical home.

They are *finally* saving for retirement at a clip of $2,500 per month *(20 percent of their income!)*, of which $9,250 per year is directed to Linda's 401(k) plan (established in 1993) and saving approximately $3,000 per year on taxes.

Jimmy Buffett will have to wait; Linda and Michael are having too much fun building their cash cow.

Pat and Ruth's Cut the Fat Worksheet

| | Reduction Amount | | | |
	Annual	Monthly	Yearly	Strategy
Fixed Expenses:				
Taxes	$ 30,000	$ 250	$ 3,000	Sar/Sep
		12	150	Property taxes
Mortgage or rent	0	0	0	
Utilities	1,200	0	0	
Telephone	2,400	100	1,200	Reduce long-distance
Total fixed	$ 33,600	$ 362	$ 4,350	
Variable Expenses:				
Food	$ 6,000	$ 0	$ 0	
Medical	2,000	83	1,000	Join HMO
Clothing	4,000	0	0	
Home insurance	500	0	0	
Auto insurance	1,000	0	0	

Home maintenance	1,200	0	0	
Auto maintenance	1,500	42	500	Located an honest mechanic
Entertainment	500	0	0	
Restaurants	1,200	0	0	
Vacations	5,000	100	1,200	Budgeted
Gifts	10,000	500	6,000	Budgeted
Dry cleaning	600	0	0	
Life insurance	4,400	0	0	
Total variable	$ 37,900	$ 725	$ 8,700	
Total expenses	$ 71,500	$ 1,087	$13,050	

Pat and Ruth's Fat-Reduction Analysis: Pat and Ruth needed to cut from $1,180 to $2,120 from their monthly expenses. They also needed to move their existing savings into investments that would give them a higher rate of return, and they needed to start reinvesting their annual investment interest. Pat and Ruth's specific options will be discussed in the next workout: Pump It Up.

Pat's father was stricken with a stroke in 1990. Following hospitalization, he lived with Pat and Ruth for two years. However, because he required such extensive nursing care, they were forced to move him into a nursing home. They are currently spending $12,000 per year to support his nursing home care.

As frugal as they were, they finally drove their clunker into the ground and were forced to purchase a new clunker. They also found their ideal vacation home (a four-hour drive away) on the Bay, paying cash for it in 1993.

Pat and Ruth now have two beautiful grandchildren; and yes, they still save 20 percent of their income.

CUT-THE-FAT STRATEGIES

By adopting as many of the following expense-reduction strategies as possible, you will trim your expenses and enhance your investment future by leaps and bounds.

Property Taxes

Strategy 1: **Challenge Your Assessment.** The discussion for this strategy item will focus on property versus income. A comprehensive discussion of taxes will be covered in the Tax Attack Workout during Week 10.

Despite the wringing of hands and gnashing of teeth over price depreciation of most homes, property-tax bills are continuing to rise. One way to reduce your annual property tax bill is to CHALLENGE YOUR PROPERTY ASSESSMENT.

Your tax bill results from multiplying the assessed value of your home by the local tax rate. First, contact your local tax assessor's office to determine how the assessment is set. The telephone number can be found in your local directory under City/County Government. To correct an inflated assessment, you generally must prove either that the market value assigned to it is wrong or that the description of your property is incorrect.

Second, check your property tax records at city hall. There are often errors, such as inaccurate house or lot dimensions and incorrect building materials.

Remember, approximately half of all homeowners who challenge their property tax assessments by appealing to local tax authorities win reductions of 10 percent or more in a matter of months.

Pat and Ruth initiated this strategy and managed to reduce their property tax by $150 dollars per year.

Mortgage

Strategy 2: **Refinance.** Although it may delay debt freedom day, many homeowners who have refinanced have CUT MONTHLY PAYMENTS BY 25 PERCENT and slashed total projected interest costs by 40 percent.

Rule of thumb: If you can get a rate even one percentage point lower than your current mortgage and you plan to stay in your house long enough to amortize the closing costs (usually 4 percent of the loan amount), you should consider refinancing. Refer back to Table 3–7 to review mortgage payments based on different mortgage rates.

Strategy 3: **Sell Your Home.**   Sounds radical, but if you and your spouse really want to take a major bite out of annual expenses until your financial future is on firmer ground, spruce up the house, sell it, and move on to less expensive digs.

Linda and Michael found this strategy appealing. Of course, if you recall, their financial situation needed radical surgery. After the children went off to college, they purchased a used sailboat large enough to live aboard and docked it at a local marina. They had their home sold in three months, paid off their mortgage, and used their equity to pay down on the boat. Although their living quarters were reduced, so was their monthly expense for a place to call home. They went from a monthly mortgage payment and home expenses of $1,500 to a monthly slip fee of $250 and boat loan payment of $400.

This strategy allowed them to get out from underneath a huge blanket of debt in less than 18 months! Monthly savings: Approximately $850.

One word of caution: If you are lucky enough to sell your home for a profit, plan on purchasing another home at equal or greater value within 24 months to avoid paying a tax on the gain.

Strategy 4: **Double-Check Your Mortgage Insurance.**   You may be buying insurance your lender no longer demands.

Strategy 5: **Be Responsible for Paying Property Taxes and Insurance.**   Pay these yourself rather than have your mortgage banker include them in your mortgage payment. In this manner, you earn valuable interest on the savings, and your banker is not given a free ride on your money. Linda and Michael elected to pay their own annual taxes and insurance on their new home, which totaled $5,000 per year. By establishing an account that paid 5 percent annual interest, they not only paid their taxes and insurance, they also earned an additional $250 dollars.

Rent

Strategy 6: **Prepay Six Months.**   Some landlords will be willing to negotiate a discount upwards of 10 percent of your annual rent as a result of prepayment. Multiply 10 percent of your monthly rent by six months and give your landlord a call. Consider this strategy only if you believe that your discount will beat the rate of return earned if you invested this money elsewhere.

Strategy 7: **Move to a New Location.**   Consider moving to an apartment complex of comparable rental value if the owners offer competitive rates that include all utilities. This can reduce your monthly expenses by as much as 20 percent.

Utilities

Strategy 8: **Flip Off All Lights When You Leave a Room.** This may sound silly to many of you, but electrical use in the home is taken so much for granted that most of us have our homes lit up like Times Square, especially if we have children.

Utilizing this strategy will reduce your monthly utility bill significantly. Chuck reduced his utility bill by 10 percent, or $60 per year, and Michael and Linda reduced their bill by a whopping 25 percent, or $400 per year.

Strategy 9:   **Monitor Your Thermostat Setting.**   Turn down the setting a couple of degrees in the winter and raise it a few degrees in the summer; your body will adjust to the environment. Use cozy quilts for the winter and skimpy clothes for the summer.

Chuck, and Linda and Michael all realized significant savings!

Strategy 10: **Install an Electric Load Controller.**   This will conserve electricity by shutting down or lowering power to certain heavy load appliances such as your water heater.

Monthly bills for people who use an electric load controller have reportedly dropped by 40 percent!

Telephone

Strategy 11: **Decline All Telephone Service Bells and Whistles.** Stick to your basic service for local calls. Dropping two to three unnecessary features can shave $10–15 off your monthly bill. Resist the temptation to install a second line. Chuck found additional options unnecessary and dropped them all, saving $60 per year.

Strategy 12: **Be Smart in Selecting Long Distance.**   Choosing the right long-distance carrier and discount plan can cut monthly bills by 20 percent or more, provided you make the minimum number of long-distance calls per month required by the plan.

Strategy 13: **Establish a Budget.**   Friends and family may live far away, but they would in all likelihood appreciate receiving a letter from you as much as a telephone call. Linda and Michael averaged $70 per month on long-distance calls, comprising 70 percent of their total bill. They established a budget that reduced their long-distance amount to no more than $20 per month. This saved them $50 per month, or $600 per year!

Pat and Ruth managed to spend $200 per month for telephone service, of which *$170* related to long-distance calls to the kids and grandchildren. They decided to budget their calls and cut their bill in half—saving them $100 dollars per month, or $1,200 dollars per year!

Auto Loan

Strategy 14: **Buy Used.**   Since a car suffers approximately 60 percent of its five-year depreciation in its first 24 months, financing a well-maintained two-year-old car will reduce your monthly payments anywhere from 5–20 percent.

Chuck, and Linda and Michael ultimately all decided to purchase pre-owned vehicles with cash. They focused on vehicles that featured low maintenance, reliability, and long-term value. They also had a reliable mechanic check out their prospect before the purchase. Linda and Michael's mechanic, known in the trade as "Dr. Benz," was so reliable that he rejected the first 10 vehicles Michael drove by for inspection.

Independent consumer magazines are a good place to start for used car research. Chuck purchased his three-year-old, pre-owned car in 1994 for 50 percent less than he would have paid for a new vehicle.

After each of their lease terms expired, Linda and Michael paid for one Mercedes Benz in 1992 and cash for another in 1993.

Credit Cards

Strategy 15: **Reshop Your Card.**   If you are like millions of plastic toting Americans who carry a monthly balance, aggressively search for the lowest interest rate offered by a lender.

Strategy 16: **Cut Them Up!** Michael and Linda did! Carry no more than two cards for use in an emergency and pay off your balance every month.

Food

Strategy 17: **Join a Discount Club.** More than 700 retail warehouse clubs, like Sam's, sell groceries at rock-bottom prices. A 1992 study by the Food Marketing Institute found that on average these clubs offer 26 percent savings over retail competitors. Assuming you spend approximately $100 per week to feed your family, making purchases through a club will save you *at least* $25 per week.

Strategy 18: **Make a Grocery List Before You Go to the Store That Is Based around a Weekly Meal Plan.** This may sound trivial and obvious to some of you, but many Americans wander up and down a grocery aisle simply loading their cart with items that catch their fancy without regard to sales, brand names, or how they plan to work the item into a meal.

The result? You throw your money away on nonessential items and eventually throw away left-over items. This can add anywhere from $20–$30 *per week* to your expenses.

Strategy 19: **Grow Your Own Natural Food.** Pesticide-free produce has swelled the ranks of US gardeners to more than 30 million. Some have reportedly cut their vegetable and herb food bills by 30 percent. This will work for you provided you have the proper acreage, soil, and green thumb.

Medical

Strategy 20: **Quit Smoking.** Easier said than done, but the financial rewards are astounding. Assuming you are an average "pack-a-day" smoker, quitting will *immediately* net you an additional $60 per month.

Strategy 21: **Enroll in a Health Maintenance Organization (HMO).** Most care is provided for a flat fee, usually with no deductible, and copayments of $5–$10 dollars per office visit. A family of four can lower their out-of-pocket expenses by as much as $1,000 per year.

Strategy 22: **Purchase Generic Drugs.**

Strategy 23: **Schedule Preventive Medical Checkups.**

Strategy 24: **Exercise and Eat Smart.**

Clothing

Strategy 25: **Stick to Hand-me-Downs for Toddlers.** Resist the temptation to add to the $23 billion "dress me like a doll" infant market. It is not uncommon for dual-career couples to spend $500 per month on infant clothes and related items. Your child can easily get by on a quarter of the expense, reducing your expense by an additional $350 per month.

Strategy 26: **Shop Manufacturer-Owned Outlets.** You are probably familiar with the name-brand manufacturers such as Liz Claiborne, Levi's, Nautica, and Calvin Klein that operate their own independent stores, offering discounts of up to 50 percent to a hungry public.

Strategy 27: **Buy Quality, Not Quantity.**

Strategy 28: **Look for Sales.** (Linda's Mother taught her this.)

Strategy 29: **Stay Within a Budget.**

Strategy 30: **Don't Impulse Buy.**

Strategy 31: **Buy Clothes That Can Be Accessorized for Different Looks.**

Tuition/Educational Funding

Strategy 32: **Have Your Child Live at Home for One Year.** This is only feasible if he or she attends a local degreed or technical college. Annual savings: approximately $ 6,000.

Strategy 33: **Scholarships and Grants.** *Free Money for College* and *Free Money for Graduate School,* Laurie Blum, Henry Holt 1-800-488-5233.

Strategy 34: **Loans.** *The Princeton Review: The Student Guide to Paying for College* Kal Shaney and Geoff Martz, 1-800-733-3000.

Strategy 35: **Work Part-Time During School.**

Strategy 36: **Private versus Public Schools.** Private schools will double your cost.

Strategy 37: **Consider Resident versus Nonresident Status.** Nonresident status for any student will double your tuition expense.

Homeowner Insurance

Strategy 38: **Raise Your Deductible.** If you boost it to $500 or $1,000 from the typical $250, you can save 10–20 percent.

Strategy 39: **Seek Out All Discounts.** Deadbolt locks can reduce premiums by 5 percent, for smoke detectors another 5 percent, an alarm system by 12 percent, and a dual house/auto policy another 5 percent.

Strategy 40: **Purchase an Umbrella Policy.** Linda and Michael, and Pat and Ruth received credits of 10 percent for combining their auto and home insurance policies under the umbrella of one company. They also received an additional credit of 10 percent by increasing their deductible to $500. Annual savings for both couples: $145 dollars.

Strategy 41: **Don't Insure 100 Percent.** Deduct the value of the land and insure for "replacement cost"—the cost to rebuild your house if it burned or was hit by a tornado—not market value.

Auto Insurance

Strategy 42: **Raise Your Deductible.** Increasing collision insurance deductibles from $200 to $500 can lower your total annual premiums by at least 10 percent. Give your insurance agent a call.

Strategy 43: **Drop Personal Injury Protection (PIP).** Most health insurance policies cover the same benefits as PIP, so you're paying for the same coverage twice. Confirm coverage with your health insurance carrier and pull the plug on PIP, which could save you up to 15 percent on premiums.

Strategy 44: **Shop for Rates Before Purchasing Your Next Vehicle.**   The vehicle make and model will have a significant impact on your auto premium; generally, the sportier the wheels, the higher the premiums.

Home Maintenance

Strategy 45: **Do It Yourself.**   Part of the beauty of homeownership is taking the time to keep it maintained rather than sloughing off the responsibility to a private service.

For example: *Canceling your lawn service* will save you over $500 per year. A single family homeowner with approximately 2,500 square feet of yard will pay around $50 a month for a service to apply preemergent, weed control, and fertilizer. You can apply the same wonder drugs to your lawn in less than an hour for less than $20 per *quarter*. Annual savings: $520. Michael and Linda canceled their service, saving them a net amount of $180 per year.

For example: *Canceling your maid service* will save you over $600 per year. Most maid services charge by the hour, with the going rate (outside of New York City) around $25 per hour. Assuming two cleanings per month, spending approximately one hour to clean, you are shelling out at least $50 a month. For approximately $15, you can buy enough cleaning supplies to last you six months. The big question is, who will do the bathrooms?

For example: *Canceling your insect/bug control service* will save you close to $500 per year. Most of the leading pest control outfits lock you into a 12-month service agreement for approximately $40 a month. Barring any difficult insect control problems such as carpenter ants or runaway mice, you can implement your own monthly campaign against insects with a $15 jug of bug repellant. Michael and Linda implemented their own monthly pest-control program and never saw a bug.

Auto Maintenance

Strategy 46: **Use a Lube Service to Change Your Oil.**   In about 20 minutes and for about $20, you can once again be rolling down the highway with clean oil. Doing this four times a year will take about 80 minutes and cost approximately $80.

Strategy 47: **Find a Reputable Mechanic.** Find your own "Dr. Benz" of auto repair. This champion of metric sockets, head gaskets, and colorful jokes is usually found by word of mouth (neighbors, relatives, or friends at work), a search worth its weight in gold. An honest and straightforward mechanic will reduce your annual repair bills by thousands. A less than honorable repair facility will have you shelling out more dollars than it takes to retire the national debt.

Strategy 48: **Just Say No to Premium Gasolines.** According to the leading consumer report magazines, your car will not know the difference between $1.19 regular unleaded and $1.40 premium. However, your wallet will know by the savings of as much as $75 per year.

Entertainment

Strategy 49: **Wait for the Video.** If you're like most Americans, you're in love with the silver screen of Hollywood and have this burning desire to view the latest blockbuster upon its arrival at your local theater. A family of four will conservatively spend $50 on a night out at the movies.

Assuming once a week, you're looking at $200 per month. Wait for the fanfare of the latest hit to die down and in no time (usually 2–3 months) plop down $3 for the same movie at your video store. Annual savings: in excess of $2,000! Of course, you will have to pop your own bucket of corn.

Strategy 50: **Attend Community-Sponsored Events.** Particularly during the pleasant months of summer, plan at least one monthly event with your children. Events such as festivals, picnics, and fairs are usually free to attend and inexpensive for a family of four. Also, check out your local library for video rentals and children's programs and activities.

Restaurants

Strategy 51: **Play Chef More Often.** Dining out is another American pastime that quickly eats away at your wallet. A family of four can easily drop $75 at an average local restaurant.

Although it's good to support your local economy, a trip once a week to Louigi's can set you back over $300 per month. If dining out is a must, try to cut back your splurge to every other week; this will produce an immediate savings of $1,800 per year.

Strategy 52: **Leave Your Credit Cards at Home.**   Vow to pay for the meal in cash. You will be less inclined to order the top-shelf entries if you have placed a self-imposed, cash limit on your spending. Rather than ordering the $24.95 surf and turf, you will find yourself enjoying the $8.99 blue-plate special just as much. Additional savings: at least $60 per month.

Strategy 53: **Brown-Bag Your Lunch.**   This will produce immediate savings of at least $100 per month! And don't forget that vending machines where you buy that can of soda or candy bar can really add up. Two cans of pop a day at 50¢ each can easily add up to $25 per month or $300 per year.

Vacations

Strategy 54: **Travel Locally.**   Family theme parks are popping up all over America with discounts, savings, and entertainment value that will rival any lunch with Cinderella. Estimated savings: thousands.

Strategy 55: **Use Vacation Packages.**

Strategy 56: **Drive Rather Than Fly.**

Strategy 57: **Save on the Hotel: Stay with Family.**

Strategy 58: **Camp under the Stars.**

Strategy 59: **Seek out Bed and Breakfasts.**   Chuck cut his vacation expenses by $1,200, or 60 percent, by using the above strategies.

Michael and Linda were forced to cut their vacation budget to the bone. They allocated $500 for one summer vacation blowout. It turned out to be a family camping trip for 10 days at the local campground (At least they had a pool.) They obviously planned to increase this budget once their financial situation was under control . . . like the following summer. The family also made more trips to the grandparents for quick "gotta get outta here" weekends.

Pat and Ruth cut their vacation expenses by $1,200 per year, or 24 percent, by using vacation packages and budgeting $200 per day. They continued to vacation three weeks per year.

Club Memberships

Strategy 60: **Barter.**   At health clubs, if you can volunteer to clean equipment or teach an exercise class, many clubs will award you annual or reduced membership, saving approximately $1,500 in dues.

Strategy 61: **Join Your Local YWCA/YMCA.**   Chuck did and saved a fortune.

Strategy 62: **Exercise at Home.**   Michael and Linda canceled their club membership and developed a home-exercise program that saved them $600 per year.

Gifts

Strategy 63: **Give of Yourself.**   Consider nonfinancial gifts for your relatives and friends. Instead of spending $40 dollars on a sweater, offer to spend a weekend baby-sitting a child or catering (not purchasing) a dinner or giving a golf lesson.

Strategy 64: **Plan Ahead.**   Purchase a gift in the off-season for substantial savings.

Strategy 65: **Don't Impulse Buy.**

Strategy 66: **Make a Gift.**   Consider giving a cannister of homemade candy or a hand-made craft item.

Strategy 67: **Use a Gift Budget.**   This was an area where all three households cut back, especially Pat and Ruth, and Linda and Michael. Each couple purchased an excessive number of gifts for their children, particularly at Christmas. They really needed to get a grip. Not one of them realized how much cash they were spending. To slow down this runaway train, they committed to spend only "x" amount of dollars per person.

Strategy 68: **Give to Qualified Nonprofits.**   Make donations to your church or local homeless shelter/food bank. Clothes and furnishings are always in demand—and all are tax deductible. Be certain to obtain a receipt for your records.

Dry Cleaning

Strategy 69: **Buy Washables.**   Considering that many silks and delicate materials can't be tossed in the washer, dry-cleaning costs can double or triple the purchase price of clothing. A *Money* magazine poll found that a pair of $85 dollar wool slacks required $80 dollars worth of cleaning bills for a year's wear, assuming 20 dry-cleaning trips.

Linda and Michael reduced their dry-cleaning and laundry bill by $600 per year, or 50 percent, by laundering Michael's cotton washables and by drastically reducing the frequency of their dry-cleaning trips. As for Michael, he learned how to iron.

CONGRATULATIONS!

You have successfully completed the painful task of cutting unnecessary expense items from your daily life. We are certain that after having reviewed the 69 strategies of cutting the fat, you now have a SECURE GRIP ON YOUR SPENDING.

It is now time for you to BOOST YOUR EARNING POWER by moving on to your next exercise in the *Wealth Workout* program, a two-week process that will PUMP UP your fiscal body through the selection of various investment options.

Weeks 6 & 7
PUMP IT UP

WEEKS
6 & 7

PUMP IT UP

Weeks 6 and 7 Warm-Up Exercise:

1. Sit up tall on the edge of a chair with knees bent, buttocks tight, and feet flat on the floor.

2. Double-checking your alignment, grasp your pen and with firm steady strokes summarize on this worksheet how you plan to allocate your investments.

3. Breathe deeply and in a controlled manner as you begin to feel your heart race over the thoughts of a new bass boat docked at your new vacation home.

4. Pause momentarily, forget the guilt, and refocus your gaze on your worksheet. Repeat as necessary to complete the exercise.

Pump It Up Worksheet
as of _____

Investment Personality: Conservative ____

Moderate ____

Aggressive ____

Goals	Time Horizon (Years to Goal)	Investment Options	Historical Rate of Return
_____	_____	_____	_____
_____	_____	_____	_____
_____	_____	_____	_____
_____	_____	_____	_____
_____	_____	_____	_____
_____	_____	_____	_____
_____	_____	_____	_____

The time has arrived for you to PUMP UP your fiscal body, to select INVESTMENT OPPORTUNITIES that will increase your wealth to fund your financial goals and dreams!

However, before we begin our walk through the financial candy store, CONGRATULATIONS ARE IN ORDER TO YOU FOR REACHING THE MIDPOINT OF THE WEALTH WORKOUT PROGRAM.

> **There is no security in this life. There is only opportunity.**
> *Douglas MacArthur*

You have identified where you are financially, have clarified your financial goals, and have determined how much you must first pay yourself to achieve those goals.

This is the week when you truly begin to feel like an investor, like you're part of the game, like your money is actually going to work for *you*.

The next two weeks of pumping up your investment options will be akin to a health-cluber examining the available options to pump up for a workout routine, such as, selecting from free-weights, an aerobic program, rowing, swimming, jogging, dunking for doughnuts, whatever. Also, you will consider the question of *how long* one should engage in a particular option and *what to expect* in terms of results.

As you have noticed from your Pump It Up Worksheet, you will be asked to summarize how you plan to allocate your money among the various investment options. The worksheet contains four headings: Goals, Time Horizon, Investment Options, and Historical Rate of Return.

The worksheet will first ask you to answer one of the most important questions that will drive your investment portfolio: WHAT IS YOUR "INVESTMENT PERSONALITY"? Conservative? Moderate? Aggressive?

Before we explore the issues surrounding this critical question, it will be helpful for you to quickly examine how Chuck, Linda and Michael, and Pat and Ruth allocated their money among the many investment options by reviewing their Pump It Up Worksheets.

————————————| **Do This Now** |————————————

Transfer your Goals and Time Horizon from your Financial
Goals Worksheet in Exercise 1 to your Pump It Up Worksheet
before continuing with this workout. You can easily prepare your
worksheet by referring to Tables 5–2 and 5–3, which will provide
you with the ideal investment option and historical rate of return.

Chuck's Pump It Up Worksheet

Investment Personality: Conservative _____

Moderate _____

Aggressive   X

Goals	Time Horizon (Years to Goal)	Investment Options (From Table 5–2)	Historical Rate of Return (From Table 5–3)
Emergency fund	3	Money market fund	3.7 %
New furniture	3	Money market fund	3.7
New car	5	Balanced fund	12.2
Condo	10	Large cap stock fund	10.2
Retirement	30	Small cap stock fund	12.2

Chuck moved his liquid assets from his checking and savings
accounts to a money market fund. The money he started to save
monthly for his car and condo were invested in a balanced fund
and a large cap stock fund. The strategy he used to invest his
retirement nest egg is addressed in the next two workouts,
Reward Yourself and Tax Attack.

Linda and Michael's Pump It Up Worksheet

Investment Personality: Conservative _____

Moderate   X

Aggressive _____

Goals	Time Horizon (Years to Goal)	Investment Options (From Table 5–2)	Historical Rate of Return (From Table 5–3)
Emergency fund	5	Money market fund	3.7 %
College fund	3, 4	S-T corporate bond fund	8.5

Car	5	S-T corporate bond fund	8.5
Boat	10	Balanced fund	12.2
Retirement	30	Large cap stock fund	10.2

Linda and Michael moved their liquid assets from their checking account to a money market fund. The money they saved monthly for the children's college education was invested in a limited maturity (short-term) corporate bond fund because they only had three to four years before they would need the money. Other good options for college funding, in addition to mutual funds, include zero coupon bonds and U.S. savings bonds. These options are listed in Appendix B, Investment Options.

Money saved for their cars was also invested in a limited maturity bond fund. Linda and Mike ended up buying their boat sooner than 10 years and financed the purchase, although they paid off the balance very quickly. Linda and Michael's retirement strategies are discussed in the next two workouts.

Pat and Ruth's Pump It Up Worksheet

Investment Personality: Conservative   __X__

                             Moderate   _____

                             Aggressive   _____

Goals	Time Horizon (Years to Goal)	Investment Options (From Table 5–2)	Historical Rate of Return (From Table 5–3)
Elder care	5	S-T municipal bond fund	5.5 %
Car	3	Money market fund	3.7
Vacation home	5	S-T municipal bond fund	5.5
Retirement	15	Balanced fund	12.2

Pat and Ruth moved their liquid assets of $25,000 (emergency fund) to a money market fund from their checking and savings account. They moved the $150,000 invested in CDs to a money market fund and limited maturity (short-term) municipal bond fund (insured) to obtain a higher after-tax rate of return. Pat and Ruth's retirement strategies are discussed in the next two workouts.

INVESTMENT PERSONALITY

Before we begin to explore the information that led to the investment selections of Chuck, Linda and Michael, and Pat and Ruth, let's first examine how they determined their investment personality.

Selecting the "right" investment option (if there is such a thing) will depend on your PERSONAL GOALS and TIME HORIZON. However, your INVESTMENT PERSONALITY is the key factor that will determine the degree of zip in the portfolio you ultimately select.

INVESTMENT PERSONALITY VERSUS RISK

So far, you have developed a clear understanding of your goals and a desirable time frame for achieving them. Before you can make an intelligent investment selection, you need to clearly understand and seriously consider the concept of *risk*, and how your tolerance of it affects your investment personality.

Financial author Nick Murray believes that modern America learned the concepts of *safety*, *risk*, and *tolerance* from the Great Depression era and that we continue to use these concepts without questioning if their meaning has been altered over time.

It was the "loss of principal" during the Depression that continues to define *risk* for generation after generation of Americans.

From this experience, Americans subconsciously built up the perception that risk equates to loss of principal. This perception tends to close off the subconscious to other ways of perceiving risk.

YOUR MONEY WILL ALWAYS BE AT RISK, constantly exposed in one way or another. Consider this: The absolutely guaranteed principal of an FDIC-insured CD is at risk of losing, not its principal, but rather, its *purchasing power*, meaning a reduction in your standard of living as a result of taxes and inflation.

The rising cost of living means many people have to settle for less. You may recall that in 1972 a stamp cost 8 cents, and in 1992 that same stamp cost 29 cents. That's inflation, and it can affect your lifestyle. That is why you must have investments that can outpace inflation if you want to maintain your standard of living.

Risk is also the chance you take of making or losing money on your investments. The greater the risk, the more opportunity you have to gain and lose principal.

RISK CAN BE MANAGED AND REDUCED. Investment strategies to reduce or manage risk will be discussed in your next workout.

Your investment personality can be broadly defined as one of the following:

- Conservative: Willing to take limited risk.
- Moderate: Willing to take more risk.
- Aggressive: Willing to take major risk.

The selection of this key factor is based upon the function of your *available time* (which reduces risk), your *past experience* and knowledge of investments, as well as your *ability to tolerate* sudden swings in your investments (i.e., your ability to sleep at night).

The more time you have and the more educated you become about investments, the more risk you will be able to tolerate.

When you sit down with your trainer at the health club to put together a workout routine, your ability to reach your physical fitness goals is determined by factors that you similarly consider for your investment personality: available time, existing physical condition (experience), and personal preference (tolerance) for differing physical activities.

INVESTMENT PERSONALITY QUIZ

Determining your investment personality is as simple as answering the following six questions and adding up the score. *There are no right or wrong answers*. Simply circle the answer that is most representative of YOU.

——————————————⊣ **Do This Now** ⊢——————————————

A. How many years until you will need money to fund your most important financial goal?

0. 0–2 years

     1. 2–5 years

     2. 5–10 years

     3. 10 years or more

B. Which of the three choices below do you feel best represents the type of investment you are seeking?

     1. An investment that minimizes losses and account fluctuation in order to preserve principal.

     2. An investment that has some fluctuation accompanied by a higher rate of return.

     3. An investment that strives for the highest possible return but may have considerable fluctuation of account value.

C. A $25,000 investment you made six months ago has dropped 10 percent in value. What would you do with this investment?

     1. Sell immediately.

     2. Wait a few weeks and see if the investment turns around.

     3. Buy more of the investment. You believe this represents a good opportunity.

D. How do you feel about investing in common stocks?

     1. Common stocks should be used sparingly.

     2. Common stocks have a place in an investment portfolio.

     3. Common stocks are very attractive and should occupy a dominant position in a portfolio.

E. What rate of return do you expect?

     1. 6–8 percent per year

     2. 9–11 percent per year

     3. 12 percent or more per year

F. What "real" rate of return do you expect over inflation?

     1. 2–4 percent above inflation

     2. 5–7 percent above inflation

     3. 8 percent or greater above inflation

Investment Personality Score: _____

(Add up the numbers circled above.)

Based on your score, match your investment personality below and mark it on your Pump It Up Worksheet:

Score	Investment Personality	You
5–10	Conservative	_____
11–16	Moderate	_____
17–18	Aggressive	_____

RISK VERSUS RATE OF RETURN

Now that you have determined your investment personality, it will be easier for you to select your investment options. But before we enter into a discussion of investment options, you need to understand the relationship between risk and return.

The rate of return on your investments will dictate the amount of money and the length of time you must invest to reach your goals. Your range of investment options and their related risk factors can be summarized by the following pyramid.

Types of Investments

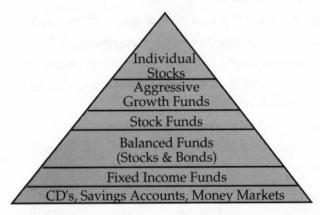

Source © CORR Software™ Ibbotson Associates, Chicago. All Rights Reserved.

As you can clearly see, there are many types of investments to choose from, with the most conservative at the base of the pyramid, and the most aggressive at the top. As you examine the various options, keep perfectly clear in your mind that THERE IS NO

ONE PERFECT INVESTMENT, AND THERE IS NO SUCH
THING AS NO RISK.

Now let's compare investment options with risk and rates of
return. Figure 5–1 demonstrates rates of return versus risk (measured by standard deviation) of different investment categories
over 19 years.

FIGURE 5-1: Mutual Funds: Risk versus Return, 1/1/76–12/31/94

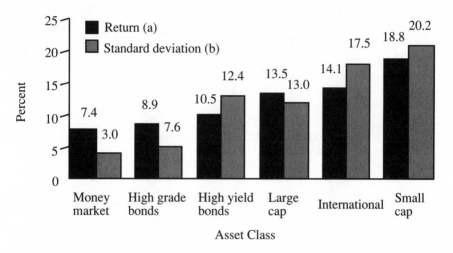

Return: (a) High-grade, high-yield, and international; Morningstar mutual funds indices;
money market; 30-Day T-Bills; large cap; S&P 500 total returns; small cap; DFA small

Standard Deviation: (b) Standard deviation is a measure of risk and volatility. The higher
the standard deviation, the more volatile the investment.

Note the obvious: THE GREATER THE RISK, THE GREATER
YOUR RETURN.

Going one step further, the greater your rate of return and time
horizon, the greater your ability to accumulate wealth and achieve
your financial goals. In a later exercise, you will learn how the
combination of various investments can actually decrease your
risk without sacrificing return.

If you save $100 per month (or $25 per week) for 45 years and
earn a 6 percent rate of return, you will accumulate $275,000. But
if you earn a 12 percent rate of return, you would accumulate
over $2 million!

You can see from Table 5–1 that the powers of time, compounding, and rate of return can make a *significant* difference in the amount of wealth you can accumulate over your lifetime.

TABLE 5–1: The Power of Time and Compounding Investing $100/Month

Years Invested	Rate of Return					
	2%	4%	6%	8%	10%	12%
1	1,211	1,222	1,234	1,245	1,257	1,268
5	6,305	6,630	6,977	7,348	7,744	8,167
10	13,272	14,725	16,388	18,295	20,484	23,004
15	20,971	24,609	29,082	34,604	41,447	49,958
20	29,480	36,677	46,204	58,902	75,937	98,926
25	38,882	51,413	69,299	95,103	132,683	187,885
30	49,273	69,405	100,452	149,036	226,049	349,496
35	60,755	91,373	142,471	229,388	379,664	643,096
40	73,444	118,196	199,149	349,101	632,408	1,176,477
45	87,466	150,947	275,599	527,454	1,048,250	2,145,469

Assuming interest and dividends reinvested.
Source: H.D. Vest Advisory Services

Now, for the last point: THE MORE TIME YOU HAVE TO REACH YOUR GOAL, THE LESS RISK OF LOSING YOUR MONEY.

Time offers you a greater opportunity to earn higher rates of return.

Figure 5–2 shows you how long-term investing reduces the risk of loss. The figure tells you that the longer your time frame, the higher probability you have of earning higher rates of return and the lower your probability of losing money. This figure makes a case for investing in stocks if you have a long time horizon.

Take a look at Figure 5–3, which shows the steady rise in the performance of stocks, bonds, and bills compared to inflation over the six decades from 1925–1992.

In studying Figure 5–3, think of any war, energy crisis, or political upheaval that occurred during this period: Pearl Harbor,

Vietnam, the oil embargo, Watergate. Note how the market responded to each of these crises: In every case, it resumed its steady growth.

The moral of this analysis is that investments can be classified based on *time horizon* and *investment personality*.

FIGURE 5–2: How Long-Term Investing Reduces Risk of Loss

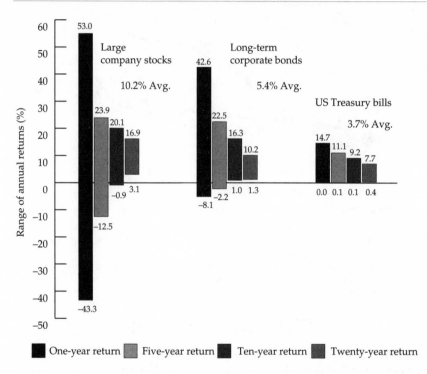

Each bar shows the range of annual total returns for each asset class from 1925–1994. History shows that the longer the holding period, the greater the likelihood of a positive return.

Source: Ibbotson Associates, Inc.

Table 5–2 will allow you to easily identify the *ideal* investment options for you, based upon your time horizon and investment personality. Identify your investment personality and time horizon and complete your Pump It Up Worksheet for investment options for each of your financial goals.

FIGURE 5–3:   Six Decade Performance of Stocks, Bonds, and Bills Compared to Inflation

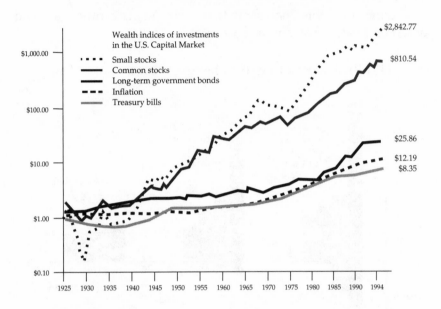

Value of $1 Investment at year-end 1925. Assumes reinvestment of income and no transaction costs or taxes.
Source: © Stocks, Bonds, Bills and Inflation 1995 Yearbook™ Ibbotson Associates, Chicago (annually updates work by Roger G. Ibbotson and Rex A. Sequefield). Used with permission. All rights reserved.

INVESTMENT OPTIONS

THE KEY TO SELECTING YOUR INVESTMENT OPTIONS WITH CONFIDENCE IS KNOWLEDGE AND EDUCATION. Rather than investing haphazardly in a patchwork of securities, take your time over the next two weeks to give your portfolio option selection careful consideration.

There are TWO MAJOR CATEGORIES OF INVESTMENTS to consider in building your portfolio: fixed-income and equities.

Fixed-Income (Bonds)

Fixed-income instruments are debt obligations issued by various entities, including the US government, municipalities, or

TABLE 5–2: Investment Options Based on Time Horizon and Investment Personality

| | Investor Time Horizon | | | | | | | | |
| | 1–3 yrs | | | 3–5 yrs | | | 5+ yrs | | |
	Conservative	Moderate	Aggressive	Conservative	Moderate	Aggressive	Conservative	Moderate	Aggressive
Money market fund	Yes	Yes	Yes						
Short-term government fund				Yes					
Long-term government fund (b)									
Short-term corporate fund					Yes				
Long-term corporate fund (b)									
Short-term municipal fund (a)				Yes	Yes				
Long-term municipal fund (a) (b)									
High-yield bond fund (b)									
Balanced fund						Yes	Yes		
Large cap stock fund								Yes	
Small cap stock fund									Yes

Source: H.D. Vest Advisory Services.
(a) Consider a municipal bond fund if you are in a high tax bracket.
(b) Consider these bond funds when using strategic asset allocation as discussed in Pump It Up Workout.

corporations. You are loaning money to one of the entities with the expectation that you will be repaid with interest.

Investment options related to fixed income all share the following two characteristics:

- Most pay interest at specified intervals.
- You are paid back the face value of your investment at maturity.

In general, the value of fixed-income investments moves in the opposite direction of changes in interest rates. Therefore, if interest rates rise, as everyone remembers from 1994, the value of your fixed-income investment declines and vice versa.

Equities

The second major category of investments for you to consider is equities, investments in common stock of corporations.

In general, equities offer you the opportunity for GREATER RETURNS THAN FIXED-INCOME, averaging 5–7 percent greater since 1920 (see Figure 5–4).

FIGURE 5–4:   Importance of Equities, 1925–1993

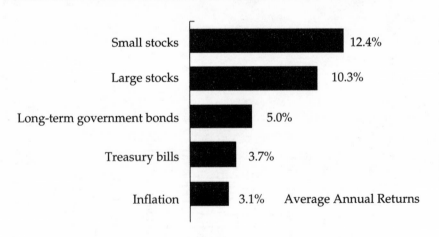

As you can see from the above illustration, equities have historically produced higher long-term rates of return, particularly during periods of economic growth, when interest rates are maintained at reasonable levels.

The reason for this is simple: When financing is relatively inexpensive (low interest rates), a company is in a position to borrow money to expand operations and to increase production, boosting its dividends and raising the value and price of its stock. A portfolio flush with equities can appreciate dramatically in this type of economic environment.

However, once again taking a look at our investment pyramid, be mindful that stocks are at the top for a reason: They offer the highest rate of return but also incur the highest risk.

With stocks in corporations, you gain a piece of ownership (i.e., equity) by buying shares of the company. Rates of return vary from year to year, sometimes significantly. However, if you can tolerate (as we discussed earlier) the temporary up–down cycle that typifies stocks, you can outpace inflation and strengthen your long-term purchasing power.

STOCK EQUITIES DO NOT GUARANTEE A RETURN OF YOUR INITIAL INVESTMENT. However, if your portfolio is well diversified and properly balanced (discussed in your next workout), the various investment options that you select will work in an integrated fashion to give you a comfortable level of protection.

A description of each major category of investment listed below is detailed in Appendix A.

Major Investment Categories

CDs	US large cap stocks
Savings accounts	Real estate
Money market accounts	International bonds
Savings bonds	International stocks
US Treasury bills	US mid cap stocks
US Treasury notes	Junk bonds
US Treasury bonds	US small cap stocks
Mortgage-backed securities	Gold and precious metals
Municipal bonds	Oil and gas
Zero coupon bonds	Futures and options
Corporate bonds	

MUTUAL FUNDS

One of the objectives of the *Wealth Workout* program is to SIMPLIFY THE INVESTMENT PROCESS in order for you to understand the financial gobbledygook that is being tossed around by the "experts."

We want you to make sense out of the maze of investment options available in today's financial market. At the same time, we want your money to benefit from professional management in order for it to generate superior returns on a consistent basis.

THESE GOALS CAN BEST BE ACHIEVED BY YOUR PARTICIPATION IN MUTUAL FUNDS. Unless you have recently returned from vacation on Pluto, you have undoubtedly heard of mutual funds, and have probably invested in one or two.

What Is a Mutual Fund?

A mutual fund pools your money together with other investors and invests in hundreds of individual stocks and bonds.

According to the Investment Company Institute, a fund-industry association in Washington, DC, 31 percent of all US households currently own mutual funds.

How Many Mutual Funds Are Out There?

As of April 5, 1995, our nation had 7,607 open-end funds, including money market mutual funds. An open-end fund allows you to continually deposit or withdraw your money at the per-share value of the fund's portfolio.

The creation of the mutual fund has allowed the novice investor to step up to the plate and take a wack at the fast ball of investments. We plan to share in this closing section of the exercise a few tips on how to hit the ball.

There Are Five Distinct Benefits of Mutual Funds

Benefits of Mutual Funds

1. Professional management
2. Diversification

3. Affordability
4. Convenience/liquidity
5. Flexibility

Professional Management.   Having professional fund managers do your investing for you is a much wiser course than investing on the basis of a watercooler tip or hunch. Your money is combined with the money of other people with similar goals and then invested in individual stocks and bonds and watched by a team of professionals who live with the markets on a daily basis.

Diversification.   You don't have all of your eggs in one basket. Fund managers spread the money over a substantial portfolio of securities, providing diversification within a certain type of investment vehicle, such as stocks or bonds.

Affordability.   You can open an account for as little as $250 and can begin an automatic investment program for as little as $25 per month.

Convenience/Liquidity.   You can buy or sell shares any business day. Funds are obligated to redeem your shares pronto! Redemption requests are processed within seven days. Should a fund have check-writing privileges (becoming a popular feature), you can have instant access to your money.

Flexibility.   Investments can generally be transferred from one type of fund to another type of fund in the same family. For example, blue-chip stock fund to a growth stock fund, or money market fund to a high-yield bond fund. This allows you to shift your investments as your financial needs evolve.

Which Mutual Funds Are Best for You?

Good question. In today's competitive market for your mutual fund dollar, everyone seems to know for certain except for you: Financial talk show hosts, personal finance magazines, and direct-mail fund advertisers all suggest the "hottest" fund for you today.

Mutual funds follow the same pyramid investment categories as discussed earlier. The fund for you will be based on your . . . come on now everyone, on three . . . one, two, three . . . INVESTMENT PERSONALITY AND TIME HORIZON!

Refer to Table 5–2 for your mutual fund options based on your time horizon and investment personality.

The major types of mutual funds are detailed in Appendix C.

Selecting a Mutual Fund

Now that you have the "big picture" of available mutual fund options, let's take a look at specific points you need to consider during the weeding-out process of selecting the best funds for your portfolio.

Based upon your financial objectives and goals, it is critical that you first *understand a fund's objectives*. Request for and examine a fund prospectus. Most are very dry and boring, but if the objectives outlined in the front do not reflect what you're after, move on to the next fund candidate. While requesting a prospectus, also ask for an annual report.

Once you have found a fund that meets your objectives and goals, open the annual report and *check out the performance graph*. The performance graph gives you a snapshot look at fund performance, comparing what happened to an investment made in the fund (less any sales load) against a benchmark such as the Standard & Poor's 500 stock index.

Next, *review the fund's holdings,* the list of securities owned by the fund. The list of holdings is the foundation of any fund, and will show you exactly where the fund is investing your money.

Learn the name of the manager (or team of managers) who handle the day-to-day operation of the fund. It is important to learn how long the manager(s) has been in the position because if your fund has a superior five-year record and the manager has been at the helm for only two years, you are dealing with an unknown.

Also, read the prospectus and/or annual report for *management's analysis* of the strategies affecting past performance and future earnings. The analysis usually explains their criteria for selecting individual investments, total return, and future strategies. In examining several funds to select as investment options, be careful that each fund is not pursuing similar strategies. It is one thing for your portfolio to be diversified but quite another if your managers have all bet heavily on the health care industry. If that sector takes a hit, your portfolio performance takes a dive.

At the front of the prospectus you will find the *costs*. Up-front sales loads are the most obvious of the costs made known to prospective shareholders. Loads are used to compensate your investment professional for providing you with investment advice. Of course, as we discussed in Week 2, you can always opt for a no-load fund. But keep in mind that you are also opting for no professional service.

Far more important to the long-term performance of your fund are the *total annual operating expenses* deducted from your account. These include management and shareholder servicing fees that are deducted *year after year*. Because the expense is assessed year after year, it creates a drag on your performance that can affect your rate of return.

On average, the annual operating expense (also known as the expense ratio) for a domestic stock fund is 1.36 percent of assets, for taxable bond funds 0.9 percent, for tax-exempt funds 0.8 percent, and for money market funds 0.6 percent (Source: *The Money Rankings*, February 1995).

Last, but certainly not least, *examine the section in the prospectus that addresses risk.* You will probably not understand the legal language used by the fund management (few professionals do), but it is worth your examination. The Securities and Exchange Commission (SEC) is in the process of searching for a simple system to communicate risk in mutual funds to investors.

Providing a designated number of "stars" to denote performance is heavily used by mutual funds today and for some investors is the only criteria used to select a fund. Unfortunately, reducing the complexity of risk to a single letter or series of stars does the investor a grave injustice.

Deciding on a specific fund based purely on the stars of past performance isn't what it's cracked up to be, simply because it is based on *past performance.*

But then again, the mutual fund companies, investment magazines, and fund-tracking services all have a vested interest in the idea. Keep uppermost in your mind when evaluating the merits

of any mutual fund that NO SINGLE MEASURE REPRESENTS
THE BOTTOM LINE ON RISK OR REWARD.

HISTORICAL RATE OF RETURN

─────────────────┤ **Do This Now** ├─────────────────

It is now time for you to complete as fully as possible the far-
right column of your Pump It Up Worksheet with your historical
rate of return for each selected investment option listed on your
worksheet (money market, large cap stock fund, etc.) Find the
corresponding historical rate of return by referring to Table 5–3
using the returns from 1926–1994, if available.

This figure reflects what has happened in the past and may not
be indicative of future results. Any given rate will vary depending
upon the goal, time horizon, and impact of the investment option
you select to get you there.

The historical rate of return is measured by total return, which
is calculated as follows:

1. **Yield**, which reflects the amount of interest received on your
   fixed-income investments or stock equity dividends,
   plus/minus
2. **Appreciation** (less depreciation), which is the
   increase/decrease in the price of your shares of stock or
   bonds, minus
3. **Investment costs**, such as commissions and fees.

Taken together, yield plus/minus appreciation minus investment costs add up to total return, which reflects the total gain
from any given investment.

> Yield
> +/−   Change in value (appreciation)
> −   Investment costs
> =   Total return

TABLE 5–3:   Historical Investment Returns*

	1926–1994	1975–1994
Money market fund		
(30-day T-bills)	+ 3.7%	+ 7.4%
Bonds		
High-grade bond fund	**	+ 8.9%
Short-term government	+ 4.6%	+ 8.4%
Long-term government	+ 4.8%	+ 9.4%
Short-term corporate	**	+ 8.5%***
Long-term corporate	+ 5.4%	+ 9.8%
Short-term municipal	**	+ 5.5%***
Long-term municipal	+ 3.9%	+ 6.9%
High-yield bond fund	**	+10.5%
Stocks		
Large cap	+10.2%	+13.5%
Small cap	+12.2%	+18.8%
Balanced	**	+12.2%
International		
Stocks	**	+14.1%
Special		
Precious metals	**	+ 9.8%
Energy	**	+10.2%
Real estate	**	+16.7%

*Historical returns are based on past performance of these indices/funds and are for demonstrative purposes only.

**Data not available.

***Reflect years 1985–1994 only.

Note: We suggest you use the 1926–1994 historical returns for your worksheet, if available, as they reflect a longer time period and are more conservative.

Source: Ibbotson & Associates.

CONGRATULATIONS!

Over the past two weeks you have identified your investment personality and investment options to achieve your financial goals.

Let's face it, being a good investor doesn't come naturally. It takes work, education, and truth to sort through the maze of investment options presented to you in today's financial world. But it also takes your ability to make a decision to invest now rather than waiting for something unknown to happen in the future.

When you defer investing in great long-term vehicles because of short-term worries, you are missing the fact that your goals, as listed in Week 1, are extremely date-specific. For example, the university will not put off your son's first semester tuition payment because you decide that you want to watch where the markets are headed.

Unfortunately, this fact never becomes clear until it is too late. Therefore, you only have history to fall back on. And history really teaches us faith in the future, not fear of it.

Before we wrap up this exercise and move on to the rewards of investment strategies, keep in mind that your investment selection process can be greatly enhanced with the service provided by your personal money trainer.

Not only will your trainer help you wade through the paperwork of picking a fund, she or he will help make your life easier by taking care of the fund paperwork that is sure to follow.

Weeks 8 & 9
REWARD YOURSELF

8 & 9

REWARD YOURSELF

Weeks 8 and 9 Warm-Up Exercise:

1. Stand tall with back against a wall, arms slightly bent and extended in front at shoulder height;
2. Maintaining erect posture, lift one foot, simulating perfect balance;
3. Breathing normally, direct your concentration to the worksheet exercise firmly grasped in right or left hand, carefully examining whether your investments are properly balanced;
4. Repeat repetitions as necessary. (This is an excellent warm-up for the taxing exercise to follow).

Rewards Worksheet
as of _____

Goals	Time Horizon	Investment Strategy
_____	_____	_____
_____	_____	_____
_____	_____	_____
_____	_____	_____
_____	_____	_____

Investment Personality: _____

Strategic Asset Allocation:

Portfolios:	Greater than $100,000	Less than $100,000	
	_____	_____	Stocks
	_____	_____	Bonds
	_____	_____	International
	_____	_____	Real estate
	_____	_____	Energy
	_____	_____	Precious metals
	100%	100%	

Now is when you begin to pull together all of your work over the past seven weeks by selecting INVESTMENT STRATEGIES that will help you achieve your financial goals.

> **Let us be thankful for the fools; but for them, the rest of us could not succeed.**
>
> *Mark Twain*

In your previous workout, you identified investment options for each of your financial goals. Options for goals shorter than five years are generally straightforward and limited. But for goals longer than five years (such as retirement) there are many more choices. The strategies in this workout will help you further define your investment options for these long-term goals.

FOUR INVESTMENT STRATEGIES

The *Wealth Workout* program will discuss four simple strategies that have proven successful over time:

- Strategic asset allocation.
- Diversification.
- Dollar-cost averaging.
- Buy-hold.

From a practical point of view, we will also discuss how each of our three households implemented each strategy according to their financial goals. Now is the time to pull the Rewards Worksheet from the beginning of this chapter. Below, you will see how each of our households prepared their worksheets. Then we will walk you through each strategy so you can fill in your worksheet.

Chuck's Rewards Worksheet

Goals	Time Horizon (Years)	Investment Strategy
Car	5	Monthly dollar-cost averaging Diversification (mutual funds)
Condo	10	Monthly dollar-cost averaging Diversification (mutual funds)
Retirement	30	Monthly dollar-cost averaging Strategic asset allocation, Buy-hold

Investment personality: Aggressive
Strategic asset allocation: (from Table 6–1)

Portfolios:	Greater than $100,000	Less than $100,000	
	38%	40%	Stocks
	10	10	Bonds
	36	40	International
	5	0	Real estate
	5	0	Energy
	6	10	Precious metals
	100%	100%	

Linda and Michael's Rewards Worksheet

Goals	Time Horizon (Years)	Investment Strategy
Education	3–4	Monthly dollar-cost averaging Diversification (mutual funds)
Cars	5	Monthly dollar-cost averaging Diversification (mutual funds)
Boat	10	Monthly Dollar Cost Averaging Diversification (mutual funds)
Retirement	25	Monthly dollar-cost averaging Strategic asset allocation, Buy-hold

Investment personality: Moderate
Strategic asset allocation: (from Table 6–1)

Portfolios:	Greater than $100,000	Less than $100,000	
	28%	25%	Stocks
	35	35	Bonds
	26	30	International
	3	0	Real estate
	3	0	Energy
	5	10	Precious metals
	100%	100%	

Pat and Ruth's Rewards Worksheet

Goals	Time Horizon (Years)	Investment Strategy
Elder care	5	Diversification (mutual funds)
New car	3	Diversification (mutual funds)
Vacation home	5	Diversification (mutual funds)
Retirement	15	Monthly dollar-cost averaging Strategic asset allocation Buy-hold

Investment personality: Conservative

Strategic asset allocation: (from Table 6–1)

Portfolios:	Greater than $100,000	Less than $100,000	
	17%	20%	Stocks
	60	57	Bonds
	16	13	International
	2	0	Real estate
	2	0	Energy
	3	10	Precious metals
	100%	100%	

Now, let's talk about each strategy:

STRATEGIC ASSET ALLOCATION

It is a well-known fact that some asset classes (equities, bonds, etc.) thrive in economic climates where others falter. The predictability of this fact is *critical* to your long-term investment approach.

One widely accepted strategy that provides rather predictable results is strategic asset allocation. The strategy is quite simply a process where you decide what percentage of your money is divided into different investment-class *categories*.

YOUR ASSET ALLOCATION IS CONSIDERED BY MOST RESPECTED ADVISORS TO BE THE MOST FUNDAMENTALLY IMPORTANT DECISION THAT YOU AS AN INVESTOR WILL MAKE. The allocation process involves investing in different asset *categories* to achieve a long-term level of diversification that allows you to sleep at night (reduces risk) and gives you the advantage of higher returns, which allows you to achieve your long-term dreams.

Recent studies suggest that as a long-term investor, you would benefit greatly by focusing on the allocation among asset *categories* rather than worrying about selecting individual investments.

MORE THAN 90 PERCENT OF PORTFOLIO PERFORMANCE IS DETERMINED BY ASSET ALLOCATION STRATEGY. Less than 10 percent of performance is derived from the specific investments within the portfolio.[1]

OK, How Should My Asset Categories Be Split?

If you are seeking a general rule of thumb for asset allocation, Table 6–1 will be useful.

TABLE 6–1:   Strategic Asset Portfolio Percentage Allocation

| Investment Personality: | For account values greater than $100,000 | | |
	Conservative	Moderate	Aggressive
Bonds	**60%**	**35%**	**10%**
High-grade*	45	20	0
High-yield	15	15	10
Stocks	**17**	**28**	**38**
Large cap	7	11	15
Small cap	10	17	23
International	**16**	**26**	**36**
Stocks	16	26	36
Special	**7**	**11**	**16**
Precious metals	3	5	6
Energy	2	3	5
Real estate	2	3	5

[1] Studies conducted by Gary P. Bronson, L. Randolph Hood, and Gilbert L. Beebower, "Determinants of Portfolio Performance," *Financial Analysts Journal*, July/August 1986. "Determinants of Portfolio Performance II," May/June 1991.

Investment Personality:	For account values less than $100,000		
	Conservative	Moderate	Aggressive
Bonds	57%	35%	10%
High-grade*	21	20	0
High-yield	36	15	10
Stocks	20	25	40
Large cap	10	10	17
Small cap	10	15	23
International	13	30	40
Stocks	13	30	40
Special	10	10	10
Precious metals	10	10	10

*Tax-free funds should be considered if you are in a high tax bracket.

Source: H.D. Vest Advisory Services.

Through asset allocation, you spread your assets among various asset categories in order to create an optimal portfolio of investments that react differently to various market conditions. The result: You take on as little risk as necessary to achieve your expected rate of return.

Notice in Table 6–2 how all six asset categories performed over the past 20 years. Also notice the "Composite" line on the graph, which represents the asset allocation portfolio. It has the third highest performance of any of these asset classes over the past 20 years while demonstrating relatively little volatility (peaks and valleys).

When all is said and done, it is likely that one category will have been a disappointment, another will have hit a home run, and still another will be a pleasant surprise. The point here is that your portfolio has a higher probability of experiencing positive growth because it is *properly allocated*.

Chuck, Linda and Michael, and Pat and Ruth used the *asset allocation strategy* from Table 6–1 that fit their investment personality.

If you desire additional assistance with the allocation-strategy process, keep in mind that your personal money trainer can introduce you to a service that measures your tolerance for risk and investment time horizon. You will be provided a customized asset-allocation portfolio recommending asset allocation percentages

TABLE 6–2: Asset Allocation Portfolio
20–Year Asset Class Performance History

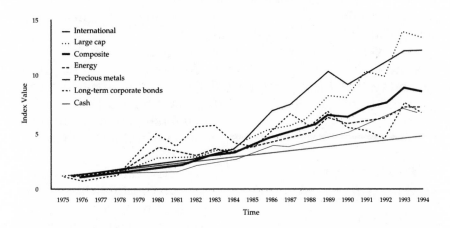

This chart is for illustration purposes only. These returns should not be considered indicative of future performance.

Source: Ibbotson Associates, Inc.

and specific investments. The service includes monitoring and reporting as well as recommendations for rebalancing and changes to the strategy and/or investments based on changes in your life or in the markets.

⊣ Do This Now ⊢

On your Rewards Worksheet, list the asset allocation percentages applicable to your investment personality. Once you have accumulated $10,000 in investment assets, you can begin the allocation process. Seasonal evaluations and annual reviews with your personal money trainer will help to track your asset accumulation.

DIVERSIFICATION

Provided that you have settled on a specific allocation percentage for each asset category, it is time for you to focus on providing *diversification for each individual category.*

This particular investment strategy is the one that makes up for your loss of not owning a crystal ball, you know, the legendary object of clarity and vision into the future. All of us instinctively know without reminder that no one can predict the market for tomorrow, much less for next year.

However, considering the doom and gloom of the daily business news, investors need a certain dose of comfort, a degree of reliability that their portfolio is balanced and somewhat predictable against the teeter-totter ride of the stock market.

> **Those that rely on crystal balls often wind up eating ground glass.**
>
> *Roger Ochs*

Diversification provides you with comfort, reliability, and balance.

Diversification is simply a way for you to pick a variety of different investments *within each asset category*. There are no guarantees against a loss in your portfolio, particularly when everything (as in 1994) drops in value. However, YOU ARE ALWAYS BETTER OFF IN THE LONG RUN BY OWNING MULTIPLE INVESTMENTS WITHIN AN ASSET CATEGORY THAT PRACTICE DIFFERENT INVESTMENT STYLES.

As we touched on during our last workout, the mutual fund is considered by a rising percentage of Americans to be the investment vehicle of choice. Mutual funds provide diversification, not only because of the shear number of available funds, but also because of the multiple objectives and strategies of each fund.

A mutual fund will invest in hundreds of individual bonds and stocks. Basically, you are not putting all your eggs in one basket.

Mutual funds are an excellent vehicle for you to use to achieve diversification, particularly for small investment amounts that are not practical to allocate among all asset classes.

Chuck, Linda and Michael, and Pat and Ruth diversified by investing in mutual funds, both for their monthly dollar-cost averaging programs and within their strategic asset-allocation program.

––––––––––––––––| **Do This Now** |––––––––––––––––

Review your investment options from the previous workout. Indicate on your Rewards Worksheet whether you will use diversification as an investment strategy.

DOLLAR-COST AVERAGING

Now that you have your investment dollars divided by category and each category is properly diversified, it is time for you to consider how you plan to introduce those dollars into the market. A classic form of introduction that will allow you to sleep at night is *dollar-cost averaging*, or DCA.

DCA is an automatic investment strategy that invests a predetermined, fixed amount of money on a monthly or quarterly basis through the use of bank drafts. The key word here is *automatic*, with DCA providing a regular, steady, and disciplined approach to long-term investing.

By investing equal amounts of money at regular intervals, your money will *buy more shares when the price is low* and buy *fewer* shares when the price rockets. In other words, you are purchasing shares with higher value.

Let's use the following illustration as an example.

AUTOMATIC INVESTING

	Investment Amount	Share Price	Shares Purchased
January	$ 100.00	$ 10.00	10
April	100.00	12.50	8
July	100.00	5.00	20
October	100.00	10.00	10
	$ 400.00	$ 37.50	48

Average share price: $9.38 ($37.50 ÷ 4)

Your average cost per share: $8.33 ($400 ÷ 48)

Say you decide to invest $100 four times per year. Your investments are made to your selected mutual funds in January, April,

July, and October. As the table shows, one share costs $10 in January. Therefore, your January $100 dollar investment buys you 10 shares. In April, the price has nudged up to $12.50, which means your $100 only buys you eight shares.

As you can see, when the price is high you are buying fewer shares. Along comes the summer heat of July and the market goes "on sale," dropping the price of a single share to $5. Because of this, your July investment buys you 20 shares. October rolls around and the price returns to $10 per share, which nets you another 10 shares.

As evidenced by this simple example, YOUR AVERAGE COST PER SHARE WAS LOWERED FROM $9.38 TO $8.33 BECAUSE OF THE STRATEGY OF DOLLAR-COST AVERAGING.

Each of our three households utilized this strategy. Since each planned to save monthly, they either wrote a check or established an automatic bank draft with a specific mutual fund. This was a great way for them to save on a monthly basis—providing them with the discipline that is necessary to save, while taking advantage of the benefits that DCA offers by investing fixed amounts at regular intervals.

Dollar-cost averaging does not guarantee a profit or protect against a loss in a declining market, but the strategy will offer you the following:

- Automatic investing, which equates to discipline.
- Satisfaction—no more sleepless nights in Seattle.

———————————————| **Do This Now** |———————————————

Indicate on your Rewards Worksheet for each goal whether you will use DCA as an investment strategy.

BUY-HOLD

IN THE LONG RUN, THE DIRECTION OF STOCK PRICES IS ALWAYS UP. THE LONGER YOU CAN STAY THE COURSE, THE MORE ASSURANCE YOU HAVE OF MAKING MONEY.

This fourth investment strategy, *Buy-Hold*, can offer you satisfying returns on your investments.

After a knot-twisting roller-coaster ride in the stock market, you may be ready to start looking for a boring bank CD to settle your stomach. There are a number of good reasons you should hang on for the buy-hold ride:

1. Statistically, the longer you are invested in the market, the smaller the probability of incurring a loss.

2. Most market gains tend to come in sudden spurts, often when least expected. If you sit on the sidelines, you run the risk of missing the upsurge.

3. You are unlikely to exit the market before the downdraft.

4. Market timing is a losing proposition. No one person or method has been able to call major market moves and interest rate changes with sufficient accuracy to justify paying market-timing fees.

5. Asset allocation and diversification are the best strategies to obtain acceptable levels of returns while reducing the risks and volatility that cause us to jump out of the market at the wrong time, every time.

STILL FEEL YOU CAN TIME THE MARKET? Here is a look at the kind of risk you are taking. Had you simply invested in stocks and held them throughout the entire decade of the 1980s, your average annual return would have been 17.6 percent. However, if you tried to time the market and missed only the 40 best trading days over that 10-year period, your annual return dropped to just 4 percent. This is an investment loss of 13.6 percent when missing an average of only four trading days a year. Since no one knows in advance when the "best" days will be, the obvious advice to investors is BE INVESTED AND STAY INVESTED.

What you DON'T want to do is slip into the market for six months (particularly after your efforts with *Wealth Workout*), exit stage right for the next three, and then decide to slide your way back in. Instead, do this:

• Don't wait for the perfect time to invest.
• Use an automatic investment program.
• Remain focused on your goals.
• Disregard the market potholes.

---------------------------| **Do This Now** |---------------------------

Indicate on your Rewards Worksheet each goal that you are committed to the buy-hold strategy. This commitment will help you through the tough times and reward you in the good times.

CONGRATULATIONS!

You have identified the investment strategies that can help you achieve your financial goals.

While the above strategies will help you achieve your goals, the strategies we will talk about in the next workout will reduce your taxes and at the same time further enhance your ability to retire with the money you need for a wonderful and fulfilling retirement. So, on to the TAX ATTACK.

1040

Week 10
TAX ATTACK

TAX ATTACK

Week 10 Warm-Up Exercise:

1. Maintaining good posture with shoulders relaxed, abs tight, bend both elbows and clench both fists;
2. With alternating and accelerating upward-downward motion, profusely pound last year's tax return strategically positioned before you, pause briefly taking three deep breaths, resume exercise;
3. Repeat reps.

Tax Attack Worksheet
as of _____

Tax Strategies	Amount	Tax Savings
Municipal tax-free bonds	$ _____	$ _____
IRAs	_____	_____
401(k)	_____	_____
403(b)	_____	_____
Annuities	_____	_____
SEP	_____	_____
Keogh	_____	_____

In today's climate of frustration with the politics of Washington, Americans are *finally* getting through to the body of persons that constitute the governing authority of our nation with the message OUR TAXES ARE TOO HIGH; GIVE US SOME RELIEF!

According to a recent study released by the nonpartisan research group, Tax Foundation, based in Washington, DC, the median household (working couple with two children, gross income of $53,354) now pays 39.5 percent of its gross income in federal, state, and local taxes. Households in the top 39.6 percent federal tax bracket are paying close to 50 percent of their gross income in federal, state and local taxes. Here's the kicker: At this rate, these individuals could end up paying as much as *$4.2 million* in taxes during their productive years.

Imagine what could be done with that hard-earned money in retirement.

The furor over taxes has caused a great deal of open and heated debate on Capitol Hill regarding ways to relieve the burden, with refreshing ideas such as the flat tax, consumption tax, and national sales tax . . . unfortunately, the problem for your "median household" is that it will remain a debate for the foreseeable future.

HOW TO REDUCE YOUR TAXES

Next to death, taxes will remain an inevitable part of life. Therefore, your best defense is to plan your long-term TAX ATTACK . . . a sound strategy that uses tax-free investments to avoid income taxes and tax-deferred investments to postpone the tax bite.

Our discussion during this workout will focus on ways to REDUCE YOUR CURRENT TAXES AND MAXIMIZE FUNDS FOR RETIREMENT.

The material will *not* discuss the ins and outs of completing your tax return . . . we suggest that you check-out our previous book, *Wealth—How To Get It, How To Keep It*, an excellent tool that walks you line-by-line through your 1040 tax return, turning bland pieces of information into spicey nuggets of financial opportunity.

Table 7–1 reveals that the single fastest-rising cost item from 1970–1980 was Social Security (268.7 percent), followed by personal income taxes (146.6 percent).

TABLE 7-1: Costs for the Standard Family of Four, 1980 and 1970

Category	1980	1970	Increase
Total expenses	$23,134	$10,664	116.9 %
Food	5,571	2,432	127.2
Housing	5,106	2,501	104.2
Transportation	2,116	912	132.0
Clothing and personal	1,763	1,137	55.1
Medical care	1,303	564	131.0
Other family consumables	1,109	639	73.6
Other items	957	539	77.6
Social Security	1,427	387	268.7
Personal income taxes	3,781	1,533	146.6

Source: Bureau of Labor Statistics

OK, that was back in the cultural transition period from flower power to disco. What about today? According to Chris Edwards, an economist at the Tax Foundation, taxes are still outpacing the basics in our budgets. Table 7–2 reveals that you are continuing to spend more of your hard-earned dollars on taxes.

TABLE 7-2: Taxes Still Climbing:
Dollar Increase in Per-Capita Expenditures, 1984–1994

Category	Increase
Total taxes	71%
Housing	64
Appliances	62
Clothing, shoes	61
Furniture	55
Telephone	53
Airlines	51
Automobiles*	47
Food	43
Utilities	37

* Includes gasoline and auto insurance.
The only category that rose faster than taxes was recreation, up 91 percent.
Source: The Tax Foundation.

As evidenced by Table 7–2, Uncle Sam continues to grab an ever-increasing piece of your American pie.

How can YOU reduce your current taxes? There are ways to reduce your tax exposure, but most require a PhD in accounting to understand. Americans are, after all, not educated about taxes. According to *Money Magazine* (February 1995) Americans have the following misconceptions:

- 62 percent think that people with no income must file tax returns.

- 74 percent are unaware that a $10,000 gift is totally tax free.

- 61 percent don't know the tax benefits of IRAs.

In our earlier discussions, you will recall that we dedicated a great deal of time to the subject of mutual funds. As we mentioned, mutual funds are an effective and efficient investment vehicle for most investors; they can also be a source of costly mistakes at tax time.

It has been reported that figuring the capital gains or losses on the sale of fund shares is one of the biggest sources of tax trouble for investors. Here are a couple of solutions:

1. Many of you will have your dividend and capital-gain distributions automatically reinvested into additional fund shares; this is a good long-term planning strategy.

Remember: Your reinvested dividends are taxable; do not forget this when calculating a gain or loss on the sale of fund shares.

2. If you follow our advice and utilize the strategy of dollar-cost averaging, you will end up purchasing fund shares at different prices at different times of the year. This is an excellent way to build your portfolio.

Remember: You must figure your capital gain or loss if you sold some of the shares during the year. The fund company should help you calculate your capital gain or loss.

The *Wealth Workout* program has found that the following strategies WILL REDUCE YOUR TAXES AND MAXIMIZE FUNDS FOR YOUR RETIREMENT:

1. **Investing in tax-free municipal bonds.**   Available to everyone.

2. **401(k)**.   Available to employees of for-profit businesses.
3. **403(b)**.   Available to employees of nonprofit organizations.
4. **Individual retirement account (IRA)**.   Available to practically anyone with earned income.
5. **Annuities**.   Available to everyone.
6. **Simplified employee pension (SEP) IRA**.   Available to all business owners.
7. **Salary reduction (SAR) SEP**.   Available to business owners with fewer than 25 employees meeting eligibility requirements.
8. **Keogh plans**.   Available to sole proprietorships and partnerships.

There is probably no better time to consider contacting a personal money trainer than when you begin to consider the following tax-deferred strategies to maximize your retirement funds. Your trainer will help you wade through the ever-increasing variety of investments and plans, ensuring that you have all the necessary information to make smart investment decisions.

Before we talk about each of these strategies, let's look at how each of our households used these strategies to reduce their taxes and maximize their retirement funds.

──────────────── ┤ Do This Now ├ ────────────────

Now would be a good time for you to pull out the Tax Attack Worksheet found at the beginning of this workout. We will walk you through each strategy to help you complete your worksheet.

Chuck's Tax Attack Worksheet		
Tax Strategies	**Amount**	**Approximate Tax Savings**
IRA	$ 2,000/year	$ 560/year, Earnings tax deferred
Annuity	$10,000 existing	Earnings tax deferred
Annuity	$ 8,000/year	Earnings tax deferred

Chuck calculated in Week 3 that he needed to invest an additional $247 per month at 10 percent for the next 30 years plus the $1,000 per year he is currently saving.

Chuck's Tax Attack:

1. Chuck began contributing $2,000 per year to his IRA, saving approximately $560 in taxes, and he paid no taxes on his investment earnings.

2. Chuck moved the existing $10,000 from his savings account to a variable annuity.

3. He added $8,000 to the annuity each year beginning in 1992. All earnings from this investment are tax deferred.

Within the IRA and annuity, he selected stock mutual funds, which he expects will give him at least a 10 percent rate of return over the long term.

Linda and Michael's Tax Attack Worksheet

Tax Strategies	Amount	Approximate Tax Savings
IRA	$ 4,000/year	$ 1,240/year, Earnings tax deferred
Tax-free bonds	20% of portfolio	No tax on earnings
401(k)	$ 9,000/year	$ 3,000/year, Earnings tax deferred
SEP-IRA	$ 7,500/year	$ 2,325/year, Earnings tax deferred

Linda and Michael's Tax Attack:

1. Linda and Michael continued to contribute $4,000 per year into their IRAs.

2. After the kids left for college and Linda and Michael were able to start saving more of their income, they invested 20 percent of their retirement fund in a tax-free bond fund for diversification and due to their high tax bracket.

3. In 1993, Linda's employer started a 401(k), and she chose to contribute the maximum allowable. They continued to contribute to their IRAs, even though the contributions were not tax deductible, but the investment earnings will grow tax deferred.

4. Michael, who is self-employed, started a SEP-IRA in 1994 and began contributing the maximum he could each year based on his self-employment income.

Linda and Michael invested their retirement funds in accordance with the strategic asset allocation strategy identified in the previous workout.

Pat and Ruth's Tax Attack Worksheet

Tax Strategies	Amount	Approximate Tax Savings
SAR-SEP	$ 9,000/year	$ 3,000/year, Earnings tax deferred
Annuity	$ 11,250/year	Earnings tax deferred

Pat and Ruth's Tax Attack:

1. Pat made annual contributions to his employer-sponsored SAR-SEP.
2. They also identified an additional $1,100 per month that was earmarked for retirement investment. Pat and Ruth chose to invest $11,250 per year of the amount identified in the fat-cutting workout in a variable annuity and $4,800 in a universal life policy (discussed in Week 11 Protecting Your Gluteus Maximus).

Pat and Ruth allocated their retirement investments according to the strategic asset allocation strategy discussed in the previous workout.

Now, let's briefly touch on each strategy.

MUNICIPAL BONDS AND BOND FUNDS

Municipal bonds are issued by a city, county, or state government to finance public works and projects such as schools, roads, bridges, or water treatment plants. The point here for your portfolio is that THE INCOME FROM A MUNICIPAL BOND IS TAX FREE.

That's right, the avoidance of taxes is the one and only reason that municipal bonds exist today. However, if you sell a bond for a profit, the gain will be subject to tax. An old saying still rings true today: IT'S NOT WHAT YOU MAKE, BUT WHAT YOU KEEP AFTER TAXES that really counts. Some of the highest quality, most liquid fixed-income investments you can make are in tax-free municipal bonds.

If you decide to check out an investment in the muni-bond market, *Wealth Workout* recommends you seek out solid *municipal bond mutual funds.*

Investors who purchase individual municipal bonds usually underdiversify in a couple of ways: (1) They tend to buy only bonds issued in their home state to beat local taxation; the net return is better, but 1994 Orange County, California, municipal bond investors will tell you that you're playing with fire after they watched their municipality file for bankruptcy protection. (2) People tend to buy individual bonds of the same general maturity, either very long and volatile or very short and low yielding.

Municipal bond mutual funds offer the individual bond buyer professional management, several different kinds of diversification, and efficient compounding of your dollars through reinvestment. With the help of professional management, you can capture higher yields while still holding relatively safe debt obligations.

Based on different tax brackets, the following chart shows the rate of return you would need to earn from a taxable bond investment to beat the rate of return on a 7 percent municipal bond.

Tax Equivalent Yields

Tax Bracket	15.0%	28.0%	31.0%	36.0%	39.6%
Municipal bond	7.0	7.0	7.0	7.0	7.0
Taxable bond	8.2	9.7	10.1	10.9	11.6

Your tax bracket is based on your filing status and adjustable gross income. Refer to your last tax return or personal money trainer to identify your tax bracket.

The higher your tax bracket, the more attractive a municipal bond investment would be for you. As we discussed in Weeks Six and Seven, municipal bonds are very low on the risk pyramid, particularly if the bonds are insured.

A closing note to remember with muni-bonds: In states that levy state income taxes, you have to pay state taxes on earnings if you buy another bond from another state. The same holds true if you buy shares of a tax-free bond fund that invests in other states' bonds.

401(K) PLANS

Let's continue our examination of tax-deferred strategies by reviewing the most popular investment vehicle, the 401(k).

For the sake of simplicity, convenience, and tax-deferring benefits, its tough to beat a 401(k) plan or its sister, the 403(b) for nonprofit organizations.

The popularity of the 401(k) plan speaks for itself in sheer numbers. According to Windsor, Connecticut based Access Research, 401(k) assets will triple over the next decade to more than $1 *trillion* (yes, with a *T*), becoming for most Americans their largest single asset, surpassing home equity.

These plans are popular for employees who wish to defer a portion of their salary (1995 maximum salary reduction is $9,240) to avoid current income taxes while juicing up the growing lump of cash in their retirement fund. Their popularity is enhanced when the employer matches employee contributions—what a fantastic rate of return! The plan allows you to defer taxes on the part of your salary that you contribute to a special account set up by your company. You don't pay taxes on the earnings until the money is withdrawn, usually at retirement.

Employer contributions together with the employee's contributions cannot exceed the lesser of 25 percent of compensation or $30,000.

Should you contribute to a 401(k) plan at work if your employer does not make contributions? If you can contribute more to this plan than to other alternatives, such as an IRA, then it makes sense. Talk to your human resource (benefits) department to find out the maximum you can contribute under your 401(k) plan.

The following chart shows you the tax savings you will achieve based on different tax brackets.

Tax Savings from Contributing to a 401(k)

Tax Bracket	15.0%	28.0%	31.0%	36.0%	39.6%
Tax savings	$1,386	$2,587	$2,864	$3,326	$3,659

Assuming a maximum deferral of $9,240.

Corporations that offer 401(k) plans to their employees are also boosting the number of mutual fund options. For example, companies have typically offered a few options such as an index fund, a bond fund, and a small cap fund. The trend is becoming the more the merrier, with some companies substantially increasing the number of investment options in their 401(k) plans.

This increase in the number of options also has a downside for some, who pass up on the 401(k) plan altogether because of confusion, almost paralysis, when it comes to selecting a fund.

WE BEG OF YOU NOT TO PASS ON YOUR 401(K). Contact a personal money trainer before you throw up your hands and say "fuhgetit." The opportunities of participation are too great! Remember: GREATER CHOICE OFFERS GREATER OPPORTUNITY!

During your investment option examination and selection process, the first thing to do is request from your employer investment information or a prospectus. Whatever you do, don't make the mistake made by so many Americans of dumping all of your cash into "safe" fixed-income funds.

Remember, inflation will eat up any fixed-income investment quicker than a hungry termite in the middle of the forest. This is your retirement plan we are talking about. Consider stock funds and diversify, using the asset allocation strategy we discussed in the previous workout.

Because these plans were started as a replacement for the pension plan disappearing act, it is critical that you leave your 401(k) money alone, allowing it to build and compound itself.

As a plan participant, you may be able to borrow, within limits, up to half of your account value up to $50,000. DON'T; THE TEMPTATION IS TOO GREAT AND THE PAYBACK IS HELL.

Withdrawals are permitted upon reaching the age of 59 1/2; upon leaving the company; or for hardship, disability, or death. Congress is also considering adding college tuition and medical expenses to the withdrawal permission list.

The parting message for 401(k) plans is to leave them alone, diversify, and contribute each year to the max.

403(b) PLANS

In most respects, 403(b) plans resemble the 401(k): tax-deferred retirement savings created by pretax dollars withheld from an employee's paycheck and deposited into one or more investment funds selected by the employee. So how does a 403(b) plan differ?

Specifically, the plan can only be used by employees of public schools, such as teachers, and nonprofit 501(c)3 organizations, such as the Red Cross. These employees are allowed to contribute up to $9,500 annually (reduced by elective 401(k) and SAR-SEP contributions). Refer to the tax-bracket chart included in the

401(k) section above for the amount you can save in taxes based on your tax bracket.

Another difference that 403(b)'ers have over 401(k)'ers is that 403(b) employees can transfer the accumulated savings in their plans to another investment company, *without employer approval*, if the employer has *not* contributed money to the plan.

To make a transfer, the new investment company will send you a transfer form. Complete it, return it, and the company will contact the plan sponsor used by your employer. You would want to consider such a transfer if you wish to increase your portfolio diversification, lower your fees, and increase your rate of return.

One word of caution to 403(b) employees: Bone up on the formula that dictates the amount you are allowed to contribute. Some employees are putting too much money in their plans, contrary to the 403(b) tax laws. Recent IRS audits have uncovered widespread infractions, which can result in owing additional tax.

INDIVIDUAL RETIREMENT ACCOUNT (IRA)

It is a widely held belief that IRAs are no longer as popular as they were before the Tax Reform Act of 1986. The rules are complex and riddled with exceptions. It is no wonder that 61 percent of American wage earners are befuddled over the tax benefits offered by IRAs.

However, despite Congress and the IRS tinkering, the fact remains that most corporate workers will end up with one or more IRAs by the time they retire. After all, these accounts still offer a couple of profitable advantages:

- First, your contributions may be tax deductible.
- Second, all earnings from your investments in your IRA are not taxed until you withdraw them in retirement.

So where is the confusion? Let's try to simplify the issue by first examining the general makeup of an IRA. It is designed as an effective vehicle for you and your working spouse to invest up to $2,000 annually each, or $2,250 split between you and your nonworking spouse, on a tax-advantaged basis for retirement. You are eligible to start an IRA if you earn ordinary wages or self-employment income of at least $2,000.

The extent of the tax advantages depend upon two key factors:

1. The amount of your adjusted gross income.
2. Whether you are covered by a qualified retirement plan offered by your employer.

If you are not active in a qualified plan, your full $2,000 contribution can be sliced right off the top of your adjusted gross income when you prepare your tax return.

The following chart shows you the tax savings derived from a deductible IRA based on different tax brackets:

Tax Savings for a $2,000 IRA Contribution

Tax Bracket	15.0%	28.0%	31.0%	36.0%	39.6%
Tax savings	$ 300	$ 560	$ 620	$ 720	$ 792

THOSE WHO QUALIFY FOR THE FULL DEDUCTION:

- If covered by an employer plan:

   Couples filing jointly with adjusted gross income of less than $40,000.

   Singles with incomes of less than $25,000.

- Anyone who is not covered by an employer retirement plan, including SEPs and KEOGHs (which we discuss later in this chapter).

THOSE WHO MAY QUALIFY FOR PARTIAL DEDUCTIONS:

If covered by an employer plan:

- Couples earning between $40,000 and $50,000.
- Singles earning between $25,000 and $35,000.

Remember, even if you do not qualify to deduct your contribution, you can still open and contribute to an IRA. Your investment earnings will not be taxed until withdrawal at retirement.

This tax deferral is more valuable than the tax deduction, as you can see in Table 7–3.

TABLE 7-3:   How Tax-Defered IRA Contributions Build Over 25 Years

Assumes an investor in the 28% tax bracket makes a $2,000 contribution at the beginning of each year and earns 10% interest compounded annually.

Of course, you will not benefit from such yields if you are not contributing to the max on an annual basis. Make the contribution easy on yourself and work it into your monthly budget by establishing a check draft privilege with your mutual fund. In this way, your contribution is automatically withdrawn from your checking account.

OK, you approach retirement and you begin to think about dipping into your IRA to fund your trips to see the grandchildren. If you are unfamiliar (as most investors are) with IRS regulations regarding withdrawals, you risk handing over sizable portions of your money to the tax man. The BASIC RULE FOR WITHDRAWALS is that money taken out of an IRA is generally subject to federal tax at ordinary income tax rates up to 39.6 percent, as well as being subject to state and local taxes.

One way to attempt to simplify the complex rules regarding withdrawals is to think of them as being divided into three stages:

1. Withdrawals made before you reach 59 ½.
2. Withdrawals made between 59 ½ and 70 ½.
3. Withdrawals made after 70 ½.

Let's briefly touch on each stage in a general way before moving on to annuities.

Before 59 1/2

In addition to the tax paid on any withdrawal, you will pay a 10 percent penalty. For example, if you withdraw $10,000 from your IRA, you will not only owe the tax on the full amount (assuming they were deductible contributions) but will also be penalized $1,000! OUCH!

There is one exception to the 10 percent early withdrawal penalty. The 10 percent penalty does not apply when you take a consistent income stream for five years or until you are 59 1/2, whichever is longer. Consult you personal money trainer for assistance with this method and its calculations.

Between 59 1/2 and 70 1/2

Those in the middle have the most freedom and flexibility with their IRA assets: you can withdraw to your heart's content (paying tax on all withdrawals, of course, assuming they were deductible contributions) or leave the pile of cash to continue growing, tax deferred. Also, if you change jobs or retire (which is everyone's goal), you can continue to roll lump-sum distributions from the employer-sponsored plan into an IRA.

After 70 1/2

Unfortunately, after years of penny-pinching and discipline to establish a solid retirement fund, the IRS comes along and penalizes you for *not* taking money from your accounts!!

And penalize you they will, levying taxes of up to *half* of what you should have taken out but did not; this is on top of the tax you will owe for any sums not withdrawn. The IRS apparently does not want you to leave *anything* to your heirs.

The rules for withdrawing amounts from your IRA can be complex and will be based on the life expectancy of you and your beneficiary and the value of your accounts. It is best to work out a solid plan with your personal money trainer; you will need someone you can trust and who is knowledgable about retirement plans to help you zig when the IRS zags.

ANNUITIES

Annuities are highly attractive investment vehicles. They are an investment to consider in addition to the tax-deferred strategies previously covered.

In a nutshell, AN ANNUITY IS A LONG-TERM INVESTMENT CONTRACT offered through an insurance company and offered to you by financial planners, brokerage firms, insurance agencies, banks, and investment advisors such as your personal money trainer. Annuities are available in two basic forms: fixed and variable

Fixed

A fixed annuity pays a rate of interest that usually adjusts to market rates once a year. However, in most cases, a fixed annuity will offer a higher rate of return. *Be cautious* of first-year interest rates offered as a "bonus" to attract new business, only to provide meager rates for the balance of the annuity.

MOST ANNUITIES GUARANTEE A MINIMUM RATE OF RETURN of around 3–4 percent, including a "bailout provision" that allows you to drop the annuity if the rate falls below a certain level. This guarantee is made by the insurance company that offers the annuity.

If the rate does stay above minimums, you can still cash out at the risk of not only being socked a 10 percent penalty plus taxes by the IRS (before 59 1/2) but also paying the insurance company a "surrender" penalty, which can be as high as 15 percent of your accumulated earnings.

Despite these charges, MOST ANNUITIES WILL ALLOW YOU TO WITHDRAW UP TO 10 PERCENT OF YOUR MONEY PER YEAR WITHOUT A SURRENDER PENALTY. However, withdrawals are subject to IRS taxes and penalties. Consider investing in fixed annuities if any or all of the following describe you:

- You want to lock in a set level of interest for an extended period of time.
- You are older than 59 1/2 and seek liquidity in your investments.
- The prospect of having a permanent income stream at retirement appeals to you.
- You must supplement your IRA savings.
- You want to grow your retirement fund on a tax-deferred basis.

Variable

A variable annuity offers you flexibility and the opportunity to achieve substantially higher returns, similar to that of a mutual fund. *It allows you to choose how your money is invested.* A variable annuity allows you to stash your cash in potentially higher-paying investments with earnings not taxed until withdrawal.

VARIABLE ANNUITIES ALLOW YOU TO DIVERSIFY YOUR ASSETS AMONG A WIDE RANGE OF OPTIONS, including stocks, bonds, money markets, and balanced funds. Your original investment is also guaranteed by the insurance company to be returned to your heirs in the event of your death.

There are a couple of drawbacks to the variable annuity: (1) It is subject to market volatility and (2) your income stream may be unstable because the payout depends on the performance of your investments.

Consider investing in variable annuities if any or all of the following describe you:

- Portfolio diversification is important to you.
- You want the flexibility of switching your investment selections in response to market conditions.
- You want to beat inflation by earning a far greater rate of return.
- The idea of having a minimum death benefit regardless of market conditions adds to your feelings of financial security.
- You want to build your retirement fund on a tax-deferred basis.

SEP-IRA

The SEP-IRA is a simplified employee pension plan through which employer contributions are made to IRA accounts established and maintained by eligible employees. The maximum contribution is 15 percent of employee compensation to a maximum of $22,500 in 1995. All eligible employees must be covered under this plan.

Contributions are not required every year. The timing and specific amounts contributed to the plan are at the employer's discretion. This plan is great for self-employed and small business owners with few employees. All rules for IRAs are applicable to SEP-IRAs.

SAR-SEP

A SAR-SEP, salary reduction simplified employee pension, is limited to companies with 25 or fewer eligible employees. An employee can contribute up to 13.0435 percent of his or her gross compensation, not to exceed the maximum (in 1995) of $9,240.

The key difference between a SEP-IRA and a SAR-SEP is that with a SEP-IRA, as previously discussed, only the employer can make contributions to the plan; with the SAR-SEP both employer *and* employee can make contributions. This plan is also great for the self-employed and small business owners.

KEOGH

Keogh is the term for qualified plans that are used by partnerships and sole proprietors. KEOGHS ARE TYPICALLY MONEY-PURCHASE PLANS OR PROFIT SHARING PLANS OR BOTH. Under a money purchase plan, the maximum deductible contribution for the owner is 20 percent of earned income or $30,000, whichever is less. If a profit-sharing plan is chosen, a maximum of just over 13 percent of earned income can be contributed.

Although more complex than SEPs, Keoghs have some important advantages. One benefit of Keoghs to employers is that unlike SEPs, they do not require immediate vesting. This means that employees can be required to work as long as seven years before they have access to their contributions. SEP plans generally permit employees to withdraw contributions immediately.

Keoghs are well suited for employers who want more than the 15 percent contribution available from SEPs or do not want immediate vesting.

CONGRATULATIONS!

You have just completed a taxing exercise designed to show you a few simple strategies to defer your taxes for the benefit of long-term financial gains.

The message we encourage you to remember about your taxes is BE SMART AND KEEP IT SIMPLE.

Reducing and deferring your taxes should not be your only goal but one of many goals that make up your long-term financial plan, a plan that includes protecting you and your family from serious financial loss through insurance coverage, the topic of our next workout.

Week 11
PROTECTING YOUR
GLUTEUS MAXIMUS

PROTECTING YOUR GLUTEUS MAXIMUS

Week 11 Warm-Up Exercise:

1. Leading with your tailbone, sit backward and downward, planting buttocks firmly in contact with chair.
2. Raising right index finger to your temple and right thumb to chin, rest right elbow on hard surface.
3. Keeping your breathing regular, contemplate current and long-term insurance coverages, particularly if you lead an uncertain and risky life.

Gluteus Maximus Worksheet
as of _____

	Needed? Y/N	Amount Needed
Life insurance	_____	_____
Disability insurance	_____	_____
Long-term healthcare	_____	_____
Property and casualty:		
Auto insurance	_____	_____
Homeowners insurance	_____	_____
Major medical/health	_____	_____
Elder care	_____	_____
Estate planning	_____	_____

Over the past ten weeks, you have worked very hard on wealth building exercises designed to strengthen your financial future for you and your family. Your efforts will be rewarded throughout the remainder of your life as the financial goals set forth in this program turn into reality, such as attending your daughter's graduation from college or experiencing the first peaceful weekend at your dream vacation home on the Bay.

However, somewhere along the yellow brick road of life, reality can upset your well-laid plans with personal tragedy . . . it always seems to happen when you least expect it, and it always happens "to somebody else" . . .

It is therefore painfully obvious and CRITICAL for you to PROTECT YOUR EARNINGS FROM THE PAST WITH INSURANCE FOR THE FUTURE.

This exercise will introduce you to various forms of insurance protection that will probably be very familiar to you by name, but if you're like most Americans, vaguely familiar to you in terms of specific coverage.

Making the decision to protect yourself with some type of insurance is like a weight lifter using a "spotter" on a heavy bench press: Just in case something goes wrong, it's nice to have someone in place to prevent the bar from crushing your throat.

THREE MAJOR AREAS OF INSURANCE

Selecting the most appropriate type of insurance coverage in the most appropriate amount can become a dizzying proposition, not to mention a costly one.

This *Wealth Workout* exercise will throw you a lifeline by focusing on three major areas of insurance coverage: LIFE, DISABILITY, and LONG-TERM HEALTHCARE.

We will also touch on property/casualty and major medical/health.

The cooldown for this exercise will cover, in a general sense, the areas of elder care and estate planning. A specific estate plan should be discussed in greater detail with your trusted personal money trainer. If ever there was a need to seek the assistance of a trainer, it is in the areas of insurance and estate planning.

You may be shocked to learn that after all your efforts to save and invest wisely during your life, poor estate planning could mean an immediate loss of 37-55% of your total wealth to taxation when you die . . . PROTECT YOUR GLUTEUS MAXIMUS, CALL YOUR PERSONAL TRAINER. This is how our three households protected their families and their assets:

Chuck's Gluteus Maximus Worksheet

Insurance Type	Needed? Y/N	Amount Needed
Life insurance	Yes	Employer provided
Disability insurance	Yes	$ 2,150/month
Long-term healthcare	No	$ 0
Property and casualty:		
Auto insurance	Yes	Comprehensive
Homeowners insurance	Yes	Renters
Major medical/health	Yes	Employer provided
Elder care	No	$ 0
Estate planning	Yes	Will, financial, and health-care powers of attorney

Linda and Michael's Gluteus Maximus Worksheet

Insurance Type	Needed? Y/N	Amount Needed
Life insurance	Yes	$ 472,000
Disability insurance	Yes	$ 1,650/month
Long-term healthcare	No	$ 0
Property and casualty:		
Auto Insurance	Yes	Comprehensive
Homeowners insurance	Yes	80% of fair market value and personal possessions
Major medical/health	Yes	Employer provided
Elder care	No	$ 0
Estate planning	Yes	Will, financial, and health-care powers of attorney

Pat and Ruth's Gluteus Maximus Worksheet

Insurance Type	Needed? Y/N	Amount Needed
Life insurance	Yes	$ 278,250
Disability insurance	Yes	$ 2,150/month
Long-term healthcare	Yes	Standard plan
Property and casualty:		
Auto insurance	Yes	Comprehensive
Homeowners insurance	Yes	80% of fair market value and personal possessions.
Major medical/health	Yes	Employer provided
Elder care planning	Yes	Pat's Dad—$50,000
Estate planning	Yes	Will, financial, and health-care powers of attorney

LIFE INSURANCE

Life insurance has become more complex since the days when you only needed to choose between term or whole life; policy terminology and multiple policy options have added complexity to the industry for prospective policyholders.

The result? Most Americans lack sufficient knowledge of the mechanics of a life insurance policy. This fact has led to a basic misunderstanding of insurance and has led more than one slippery insurance salesman down the path of selling life insurance for someone's pet armadillo with a guaranteed payout should the little feller not quite make it across the road.

If you have been too busy putting food on the table and paying for a roof over your head to examine the fine print disclosed in any life insurance policy, take heart; there are only two critical questions that must be answered:

1. How much insurance do I need?
2. What type of product should I buy?

The answer to the first question, depends strictly upon your personal circumstances. For instance, young families just getting started typically have a very tight cash flow, high debts associated with homes, and little, if any, savings. Married couples in their middle years may be spending dual incomes and be focused on saving for their children's college education. Both of these families need to consider life insurance to protect their standard of living and cushion the financial blow if an income was lost.

Take a drink of water and consider: INSURANCE IS FOR ASSETS YOU CAN'T AFFORD TO LOSE!

Consider the following loss of income should a breadwinner die or become disabled. Let's assume the breadwinner earned $35,000 per year with a 3 percent annual increase in salary. The family would lose the following money over the normal working life of the breadwinner.

Income Lost Due to Death

Age at Death	Age 55	Age 60	Age 65
25 years old	$1,300,000	$2,000,000	$3,800,000
35 years old	1,000,000	1,800,000	2,400,000
45 years old	890,000	1,400,000	2,000,000

The loss of a breadwinner can mean millions to the family. Use Table 8–1 to calculate your life insurance needs.

Chuck needed enough insurance to cover his burial and funeral costs. He had a policy from work that would cover this need. That's all the coverage he really needs at this point in his life.

Linda and Michael needed substantially more. Each contributed 50 percent to their total income, so both needed a life insurance policy for approximately $573,000. Linda had a policy at her company as part of her benefits package. The policy provided coverage of two times her salary, or $100,000.

Because of Linda & Michael's financial situation, they decided to buy a 10-year level term policy for Michael with a death benefit of $100,000, which cost $600 per year. They did not purchase the coverage they needed. As time progressed, debts were reduced, investments increased, and the children went off to school, the amount of coverage they needed declined. They recalculated their life insurance needs annually and eventually were properly insured.

TABLE 8–1: Determination of Life Insurance Needs

	Linda and Michael	Pat and Ruth	You
1. Family income desired (use 70%)	$70,000	$52,500	$ _____
2. Less surviving Spouse income	50,000	0	_____
3. Equals income need	20,000	52,500	_____
4. Capital needed to produce income (Line 3 divided by 8%)	250,000	656,250	_____
5. Provision for final medical/ funeral costs (we recommend 1/4 of family's total annual income but no less than $25,000)	25,000	25,000	_____
6. Total personal debt (from Week 2 Net Worth Worksheet)	165,000	0	_____
7. Children's college funding requirement (from Week 1 Financial Goals Worksheet)	97,000	0	_____
8. Emergency fund	36,000	27,000	_____
9. Child care fund	0	0	_____
10. Total capital needed Sum of Lines 4–9	573,000	708,250	_____
11. Less present liquid assets (from Week 2 Net Worth Worksheet)	1,000	180,000	_____
12. Less present life insurance	100,000	250,000	_____
13. Additional insurance needs: Line 10 minus lines 11 and 12	$ 472,000	$ 278,250	_____

Pat and Ruth need additional coverage on Pat's life of approximately $278,000. Pat bought a universal life policy several years ago for $250,000 and paid premiums of $4,000 per year for this policy. He has accumulated $5,000 in cash value within the policy. After performing this calculation, Pat doubled this coverage to $500,000 and increased his annual premiums to $8,800.

You may be a bit surprised at how much insurance you need. Calm down; you are looking at a figure that covers a span of time

until your retirement. THE PRIMARY GOAL IS TO HAVE ADE-
QUATE INSURANCE TO MAINTAIN THE LIFESTYLE TO
WHICH YOUR SURVIVING FAMILY IS ACCUSTOMED.

In addressing the second question, what type of policy to buy?,
keep in mind that your personal money trainer may be able to
help you answer the question and keep you from being plucked
like a plump Thanksgiving turkey.

There are two fundamental types of individual life insurance
policies:

1. The first type of coverage, known as *term*, has a death benefit
   but no cash value.
2. The second type, *permanent*, has a death benefit and a cash
   surrender value.

Insurance premiums vary widely by company and policy. This
is where you will need to do a bit of shopping unless you use a
personal money trainer.

Term Insurance

An annual renewable term (ART) policy provides coverage for
one year at a time, renewable each year at higher premiums.
Some plans renew every year without a physical exam, while others may require an exam in the 10th year in order to receive the
lowest rate. ART is most often recommended for very short coverage requirements of one to three years or when a large amount of
insurance is needed and you cannot afford anything else in the
short run. This is the cheapest policy that provides the largest
death benefit per dollar of premiums paid and is therefore recommended for young couples. Over the long run, this policy can be
the most expensive and should be eventually converted to a level-
term or permanent policy.

A decreasing-term policy is the opposite of ART: The premiums
remain constant but the benefit declines annually. This policy is
best suited for a situation where the need for a benefit also
decreases, such as mortgage cancellation coverage where the
mortgage on your home is paid off if the insured dies.

A level-term policy has recently become an increasingly popular tool. In level-term, both the premium and the death benefit

remain constant for the duration of the 5-, 10-, 15-, or 20-year contract. This type of policy is recommended for individuals who require coverage for more than five years.

Coverage requirements for 15 years or less are typically most cost-effective if matched to a levelized premium as follows.

Years Insurance Needed	
1–3 years	ART
3–5 years	5-year level
6–10 years	10-year level
11–15 years	15-year level
16–20 years	20-year level

So what happens when the term is up? If you are young enough, insurable, and able to afford it, you can purchase another term policy. The downside is that term coverage gets more expensive as you age, and it fails to build cash value. If term coverage is no longer an option, and going without life insurance remains unthinkable, it is time for you to consider a *permanent* policy, the second major category of life insurance, which combines true insurance with a mechanism that builds cash value.

Permanent Insurance

What do we mean by *cash value*? Quite simply, it is the money in your policy after all expenses and charges are taken out plus the interest earned over the life of your policy. It is the amount, or value, that would be paid to you if you decided to "cash out." Not a wise move though. The cash value will only be a fraction of the death benefit; you will end up paying Uncle Sam his share of tax; and you will defeat the whole purpose behind this type of policy: cash for retirement. However, most policies allow you to take loans against the cash value to help supplement income requirements. Under current tax law, these loans are not taxable.

Permanent insurance is best suited for individuals who have longer coverage needs, say 15 years to lifetime, and sufficient cash flow to pay higher premiums.

Permanent life insurance policies are packaged in three general categories: WHOLE LIFE, UNIVERSAL LIFE, and VARIABLE LIFE.

Whole life policies offer the stability of having premiums and death benefits locked in for the life of the policy owner. Also, the investment component of the policy provides for a guaranteed minimum dollar return to you as long as the policy remains in force.

Universal life is a hybrid between term and whole life policies, where your premium payments are deposited into a cash account that earns a competitive rate of return. From this account, the carrier deducts the cost of insurance plus commissions and expenses. This policy gives you the flexibility to skip premium payments, provided you have built up sufficient cash value. Compared to whole life, the premiums in universal are substantially lower.

Variable life takes the hybrid concept one step further by combining life insurance with mutual funds. This policy is said to be the best of all worlds because it combines the features of a mutual fund, IRA, and savings account. The policy can be packaged in two ways: as variable whole life or variable universal life.

With variable whole, you pay premiums for the life of the policy but are guaranteed by the insurance company a minimum death benefit. Because this policy acts similarly to a mutual fund, the cash value will vary with the performance of the managed investment component.

With variable universal, premiums are flexible and based on your ability to pay as well as on the performance of the investments in the managed component. If the investments perform well, sufficient funds may dismiss you from having to pay additional premiums. If performance suffers, you will face larger premiums or a decrease in death benefits.

All this talk about life insurance, death benefits, and protection for your loved one(s) should you suddenly die gives most of us the willies, but it is wise to remember that the harsh realities of life are usually unexpected. IT IS CRUCIAL FOR YOU TO HAVE SOME TYPE OF FINANCIAL SAFETY NET TO PROTECT YOUR DEPENDENTS and to fill the gap between their expenses and your carefully built investment portfolio.

DISABILITY INSURANCE

IF YOU WORK FOR A LIVING, YOU SHOULD NOT BE WITHOUT A SOLID DISABILITY INSURANCE POLICY. This is probably *the* most overlooked area of insurance by most Americans. We have yet to figure out why *most Americans will overlook disability coverage which pays you a monthly income if you are unable to work because of injury or illness.*

This can be a very dangerous oversight. If illness or injury prevented you from engaging in your occupation, cutting off your income, it could easily wipe out your portfolio, leaving you and your family destitute. Far-fetched, you say?

Studies upon studies have proven that one out of every three working Americans between the ages of 35 and 65 will suffer a long-term disability prior to retirement. Who do you think will pay for the food on your table? Clothes for your children? The mortgage? Gas for your car? All of these expenses will continue to become due; life just keeps on rolling along. Disability is sometimes referred to as "living death."

You say your employer provides you with disability insurance. Fair enough, but you should probably visit your benefits administrator to find out if your coverage looks closer to a piece of Swiss cheese than an insurance policy. Employer policies are often riddled with holes. Some do not cover you for a lengthy period of time, and others limit monthly benefits far below what is required by your family.

When you make the choice to buy disability coverage, keep in mind that you are attempting to buy a long-term policy that will support you and your family. Select one that provides at least 60–70 percent of your before-tax earnings until you reach the age of 65.

As you will without a doubt build a sizable investment portfolio as a result of your participation in this *Wealth Workout* program, keep the cost of the policy down by agreeing to a 90-day elimination period—the time between the date you are disabled and the date you begin to receive benefits. Dip into your emergency fund to cover your expenses for this period. Your premiums will be reduced 15–20 percent!

As you shop for a solid policy from a financially strong insurer, be certain to carefully read the fine print of the contract, particularly the print that defines "disability." The most liberal definition is entitled "Own Occ," where the insurer agrees to pay you full benefits if you can't work in your own occupation as long as you remain under physician care.

The most restrictive definition is "Any Occ," where the insurer agrees to pay benefits if you are unable to work in any occupation, which leaves open the door for the insurer to demand that you take the telemarketing job at a local skin care products distributor.

OK already, you're convinced you need a disability policy.

How Do You Calculate Your Coverage Needs?

The best approach is to follow these three steps:

1. Calculate your current monthly take-home pay.
2. Total the sources of income that would replace your paycheck if you were unable to work (i.e., social security, employer disability policy).
3. Compute the gap between what you are getting and what you need.

For example:

	Chuck	Linda and Michael	Pat and Ruth	You
1. Current monthly take-home pay	$2,500	$3,000	$4,500	$_____
Replacement income:				
2. Social Security	350	350	350	_____
3. Employer disability	0	1,000	2,000	_____
Your shortfall or gap: Line 1 minus (–) Lines 2 & 3.	$2,150	$1,650	$2,150	$_____

Chuck, Linda and Michael, and Pat all need additional disability coverage. Ruth does not need this coverage, nor would she qualify for coverage, since she does not earn an income.

In selecting the best policy, be certain to pick one that is *Guaranteed Renewable*, meaning that the company can cancel *only* if you fail to pay the premiums, which is something your disability will remind you of every day.

If you are an hourly wage earner and punch a clock, you may wish to consider a *residual benefit* option. It will add 20–25 percent to your premium, but it will also supplement your income if you are well enough to go back to the job but not yet healthy enough to pull an entire eight hour shift.

A closing word of caution on the subject of disability insurance benefits and taxes: If you paid for your own individual policy, your benefits will be income-tax free; if your benefits are the complement of your employer, you will owe Uncle Sam.

LONG-TERM HEALTHCARE

The leading edge of the Baby Boom tidal wave is approaching 50 years old. As time marches on and the numbers continue to swell, the whole notion and fear of aging is beginning to come home to roost for the age of Aquarius. As many look into the eyes of their frail and aging parents, their own mortality stares back.

The offspring from the fighting men and women of World War II will continue to benefit greatly from advances in technology, medicine, and nutrition, resulting in longer life expectancies. This raises, however, an ironic fear: living an extended life in poor health.

Face up to the fact that despite all of the highly regarded low-fat foods and in-your-face exercise programs, one day you too will be old and staring back into the eyes of a visiting grandchild. The major difference between you and your parents will be the *quality* of long-term healthcare.

There is no question that the Baby Boom generation has been and continues to be obsessed with quality, independence, and having the best at all cost. Expect nothing less when it comes to the issue of being provided long-term healthcare.

Long-term healthcare insurance is designed to cover skilled nursing home care; home healthcare; assisted living; and, depending upon the policy, other outreach services for aging and disabled Americans. As you might expect, nursing home costs are staggering, ranging from $30,000 upwards to over $60,000 *per year*.

WHAT ABOUT MEDICARE?

Medicare only covers up to 100 days of very limited skilled care in a nursing home following a hospital stay. Medicare costs now top $150 billion a year and are climbing 10.5 percent annually. Experts predict that the Medicare fund will be exhausted by the year 2002, seven short years from now. THESE KIND OF COSTS WITHOUT BACKUP CAN WIPE YOU OUT!

The chances are one in four that you will spend some time as a nursing home resident by the age of 65, one out of two chances if you are lucky enough to reach 85. In other words, your retirement plan *must* take into consideration the expense of a long-term healthcare policy. Early policies from the mid-1970s to the early 1980s were trash, too often offered by companies that went belly-up, forcing policyholders to hold out a tin cup at the bankruptcy court, hoping to recoup some of their money. Policies today are far better, with fewer restrictions, improved benefits, and lower premiums.

The bulk of the long-term policies today are sold to individuals by a trusted advisor such as a personal money trainer. Remaining policies are offered to workers through an employer group plan. At this point in time, individual and group policy benefits, as well as premiums, are about the same. Most experts in the field agree that long-term care insurance premiums should be no more than 5 percent of your income.

According to the latest available figures from the Health Insurance Association of America, premiums range anywhere from approximately $350 a year for a standard plan purchased by a 50 year old to $7,500 for a "Cadillac" plan purchased by someone approaching 80.

No matter the avenue used to purchase a long-term healthcare policy, we encourage you to protect yourself by considering the following tips:

- **Read the fine print**. A long-term healthcare policy is a contract and like any contract is filled with a great deal of gibberish and protracted definitions. Carefully review the language with your spouse and personal money trainer, being certain that the policy specifically states *when* the benefits begin and *what* is covered. Some long-term healthcare policies charge extra if a client requires assistance with eating, bathing, and dressing.

- **Buy the policy early**. Experts recommend that you purchase coverage by the time you reach your early 50s. (Hear that first wave Boomers?) You will still be in top-notch physical shape. Why wait to be rejected after you have suffered a mild stroke? Premiums will also be lower.

- **Add an inflation rider.** Although most experts in the field of economics believe that inflation will remain in check for years to come, experts have been known to be wrong. A rider will insure that your benefits track the rate of inflation.

- **Care must cover Alzheimer's disease**. Be certain that coverage is specific and takes effect without the requirement of a medical diagnosis.

- **Care must be comprehensive**. The policy should cover the expense of skilled, intermediate, and custodial care in any type of facility, including a hospital, nursing home, or your own home.

Because long-term healthcare is the fastest-growing segment of the insurance industry, many of the latest rules and regulations are either in the proposal stage or very wet on the books. Therefore, DO YOUR HOMEWORK! Call your local agency on aging (found in the "Government" section of your telephone book) and educate yourself on the latest state rules. Then give your personal trainer a call.

PROPERTY AND CASUALTY

A comprehensive insurance portfolio, of course, calls for strong property and casualty policies to protect against the loss of your home and car.

When securing homeowners coverage, look for policies that provide for AUTOMATIC REPLACEMENT COST of your home. This means that regardless of how much the property appreciates, the coverage will be sufficient to rebuild your home in the event of fire or other covered losses.

Be sure to obtain FLOATERS in the policy to protect against the loss of itemized valuables such as jewelry, furs, and collectibles.

Electing a HIGHER DEDUCTIBLE can substantially LOWER YOUR PREMIUMS on both home and auto insurance policies. If you do not own your home, it is still wise to have renters insurance for your personal possessions in case of theft, flood, or fire.

Personal UMBRELLA liability policies provide EXTRA PROTECTION beyond the limits of your homeowners and auto insurance. Considering that jury awards in liability cases can reach enormous sums, umbrella policies can provide an invaluable buffer of protection for modest premiums. Figure on paying $150 annually for the first $1 million in coverage.

MAJOR MEDICAL/HEALTH

With many employers reducing and even eliminating company-paid health insurance, and with federal health care reform in the deep freeze, individuals unaccustomed to paying for this increasingly costly coverage may soon have to foot part or all of the bill.

Unfortunately, there are no simple solutions for absorbing this cost in your budget. But there are some ways to trim premiums to make them somewhat more affordable.

Consider the following:

- If your employer no longer offers attractive coverage terms, check with groups, clubs, or professional organizations you belong to. Learn if they offer group coverage and if their plans are more affordable than your company's policies.

- If you can afford to absorb part of the cost of routine medical treatment, elect policy deductibles higher than standard. Generally, the higher the deductible, the lower the premium.
- Select a higher co-payment ratio. This will also bring down overall premiums with many types of coverage.

ELDER CARE

People are living longer. This is causing elder care to become an issue for many families.

WHO DO YOU CALL FOR HELP IN CARING FOR AN ELDER? Although we live in the age of the information super-highway, information for people who care for the elderly is scattered and hard to find. The first resort for caregivers in a crisis is the Yellow Pages. Unfortunately, your fingers will have you walking in circles. The following suggestions will get you pointed in the right direction:

1. A good starting point would be to contact a program called Eldercare Locator, a federally funded network of nearly 700 area agencies on aging. The network tracks services and finance programs for aged people who live at home. To identify a specific program or service nearest your elder, call them toll-free 1-800-677-1116, 9AM–11PM (Eastern time), Monday through Friday.

2. Employers are beginning to offer private elder care resource-and-referral services. These programs contract with local private counselors to assist the caregiver with hospital discharges and home care aide. Although only a fraction of companies currently offer this to employees, it is worth a quick call to your benefits counselor. If they do not offer this benefit, encourage them to get with the program.

3. If you have the luxury of time, referrals by mail are made by a nonprofit group called Children of Aging Parents, or CAP. You can reach them at 215-945-6900, 9AM–3PM (Eastern time), Monday through Friday. (If you leave a message after hours, they will return your call, collect.)

4. Other local nonprofit groups, senior citizen centers, and hospitals are also valuable sources for elder care. Pat's father was

a World War II veteran and was hospitalized at a VA Center in Texas. The hospital social worker staff was extremely helpful in locating a number of home care options.

5. New resources are also on the horizon. One such organization is the National Alliance for Caregiving, a Bethesda, Maryland, partnership of four different aging organizations funded in part by Glaxo, a pharmaceutical giant. Provided that funding is complete, the alliance expects to offer the first national resource center for caregivers to the aged. Their office can be reached at 301-718-8444.

In addition to planning ahead for the expense of an elder care illness, it would do you good to KNOW YOUR PARENTS' WISHES regarding medical care, as well as learning about their assets, finances, and insurance. Here are a few critical tips:

1. Beyond the ethical issues, *find out what kind of day-to-day care your elders expect to receive*. Respecting their wishes gives them a healthier sense of self-respect and control.

2. As the caregiver, *be prepared to assert on behalf of the elder's wishes*. If your parent is set on living at home after hospitalization with periodic visits from a nurse, be there to fight off the authority figure who wishes to place him or her in a nursing home (if your parent is able to care for him or herself while living alone).

3. *Be prepared to carry out your elder's financial and healthcare wishes* if he or she becomes incapacitated, by drawing up two durable powers of attorney; one for finances and the other for healthcare. This will delegate to someone the power to sign documents, make healthcare decisions, and in general manage the elder's assets and affairs.

4. *Know where the following documents related to your elders are located*:

- Their latest will.
- Social Security cards.
- Life, health, and home insurance policies.
- Tax returns.
- Records relating to savings, credit, military, and real estate.

ESTATE PLANNING

Mention the words *estate planning* and most Americans think of death. It therefore stands to reason that, because we enjoy life and wish to prolong the experience, we will do whatever it takes to suppress the thought of death and hence the thought of estate planning.

> **A man's learning dies with him: Even his virtues fade out of remembrance, but the dividends on the stocks he bequeaths to his children live and keep his memory green.**
>
> *Oliver Wendell Holmes*

Just remember that the only beneficiary of your suppressed fear is the tax collector; avoiding the thought of estate planning plays right into the hands of the IRS. This cool-down section of the work-out will discuss some general estate planning issues that you should thoughtfully consider to insure that the rightful beneficiaries of your assets remain your loved ones.

In a nutshell, ESTATE PLANNING IS A PROCESS DESIGNED TO PRESERVE YOUR ESTATE by the minimization of taxes and the smooth transfer of assets upon your death. The process can be complex and expensive; it is no wonder that attorneys and accountants make estate planning the focus of their careers. For most Americans, however, the process of preserving their estate should be simple and straightforward.

Estate planning needs will vary from household to household, but we have found that all share the following:

- The need for a will and powers of attorney.
- The need to understand the federal estate tax.
- The need to keep it all updated and organized.

The objective of the *Wealth Workout* workout that you have painlessly endured over the past 10 weeks is to show you how to build a portfolio of assets that will assure you of the better things in life, a portfolio built on a bedrock of financial security. And because most of us enjoy the act of giving, we would like the fruit of our labor to be passed on to our family at the time of our death. To assure that this long-term goal is achieved, you must have a working understanding of estate planning.

THE BEDROCK OF A SOLID ESTATE PLAN IS A PROPERLY EXECUTED WILL. Quite simply, a will directs how you want your property to be disposed of at the time of your death. It also names your *executor,* the individual charged with the responsibility of carrying out your wishes. Some experts suggest picking an independent executor outside the family, perhaps a close friend, attorney, or your personal money trainer.

While your children remain under legal age, a will also names a *guardian* for them and determines how they inherit your estate. To prevent your children from blowing their entire inheritance at the age of 18, we also suggest that you insure that any assets they inherit go into a trust.

Trusts come in all sizes and shapes. Fundamentally, A TRUST IS A LEGAL DEVICE THAT HOLDS PROPERTY PLACED IN IT BY A PERSON CALLED THE "GRANTOR" (YOU) FOR THE BENEFIT OF ONE OR MORE LUCKY SOULS (BENEFICIARIES).

The instructions, management, and disbursement of the trust contents is fully explained in a TRUST AGREEMENT. Again, this subject should be thoroughly covered with your personal money trainer.

In addition to the preparation and update of your will, it is critical that you consult with an attorney to create two separate durable powers of attorney, one for finance and the other for health care.

If you become incapacitated, the durable power of attorney for finance designates someone you trust as guardian over your assets—not to be confused with the executor of your will. Your financial guardian will be there to represent your financial interests in accordance with your wishes outlined in the power of attorney document.

Your incapacitation will also kick-in the durable power of attorney for health care, a document that selects a guardian to make medical decisions on your behalf. If you wish, this document can help prevent life-prolonging medical procedures when there is no chance of recovery.

You may be shocked to learn that despite all your efforts to save and invest wisely during your life, poor estate planning could mean an immediate loss of 37–55 percent of your total wealth to taxation when you die.

ESTATE PLANNING ALSO MEANS TAX PLANNING, particularly when we are talking about the largest tax bill you will ever receive—your estate tax.

Not everyone will owe federal estate taxes. The government allows each person sufficient credit under the unified estate and gift tax to avoid tax on up to $600,000 of assets upon your death. You say that this dollar amount is way out of your league? Remember that you are in the process of *building wealth* and will probably reach this level before you know it.

When estimating the size of your estate, do not forget to include the value of any pension plan, independent retirement plan, your house, vacation property, or life insurance benefits. This forgetfulness will cost you dearly. The tax on assets in excess of $600,000 starts at 37 percent and explodes to as much as 55 percent on estates valued at over $3 million.

The effect of the federal estate tax cannot be overestimated. The tax is due nine months from the date of your death; no sweat for your settling bones, but your survivors will be sweating bullets to raise the cash to pay the tax without having to sell the picturesque home on the bay.

The payment of excessive federal estate tax can be reduced or eliminated by a coordinated strategy of estate planning. See your personal money trainer today!

Estate Planning Documents

OK, you have followed the advice of this workout and have constructed a preliminary draft of your estate plan. WHAT DO YOU DO WITH THE DOCUMENTS? As we have advocated from the beginning, GET YOURSELF ORGANIZED! Pull together all of your original documents and keep them bundled in one safe location for ready access by the executor of your estate. Some suggest keeping all original documents in your local bank safe-deposit box; just be certain to provide a copy of applicable documents to your executor and any guardians who would be affected by your death.

Keeping your estate planning documents accessible, up-to-date, and as straightforward as possible will be the greatest asset you could possibly leave to the survivors of your estate.

CONGRATULATIONS!

You have made it through Week 11. You have accomplished more in these 11 weeks than most people accomplish in their lifetime. You have one more exercise to complete—we're sure it will be a breeze. And after all this hard work we're sure you'll want to be Financially Fit for Life!

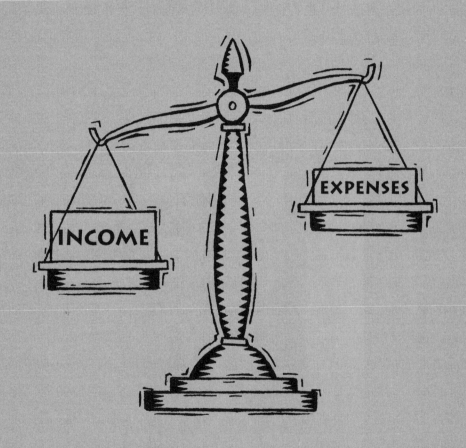

Week 12
FITNESS FOR LIFE

FITNESS FOR LIFE

WEALTH WORKOUT FIT FOR LIFE WORKSHEET

Seasonal Worksheet

Goal	Monthly Investment	Investment Option	Number of Months	Actual Rate of Return	Investment to Date

Spring Checkup Date: _____

_____	$ _____	_____	_____	_____%	$ _____
_____	$ _____	_____	_____	_____%	$ _____
_____	$ _____	_____	_____	_____%	$ _____
_____	$ _____	_____	_____	_____%	$ _____
_____	$ _____	_____	_____	_____%	$ _____

Summer Checkup Date: _____

_____	$ _____	_____	_____	_____%	$ _____
_____	$ _____	_____	_____	_____%	$ _____
_____	$ _____	_____	_____	_____%	$ _____
_____	$ _____	_____	_____	_____%	$ _____
_____	$ _____	_____	_____	_____%	$ _____

Fall Checkup Date: _____

_____	$ _____	_____	_____	_____%	$ _____
_____	$ _____	_____	_____	_____%	$ _____
_____	$ _____	_____	_____	_____%	$ _____
_____	$ _____	_____	_____	_____%	$ _____
_____	$ _____	_____	_____	_____%	$ _____

Winter Checkup Date: _____

_____	$ _____	_____	_____	_____%	$ _____
_____	$ _____	_____	_____	_____%	$ _____
_____	$ _____	_____	_____	_____%	$ _____
_____	$ _____	_____	_____	_____%	$ _____
_____	$ _____	_____	_____	_____%	$ _____

As so eloquently spoken in 1945 by Mr. Churchill, the relevance
of the quote lives on as much
today for you as demonstrated
by your commitment over the
past 90 days to complete this
Wealth Workout program . . .
give yourself a brief round of
applause and take a bow !

> **We may allow
> ourselves a brief
> period of rejoicing.**
> *Winston Churchill*

You are in the process of
completing a financial fitness
program that pulls together a tailor-made plan for your financial
future, a plan that has prepared you to enjoy with confidence

FINANCIAL FITNESS FOR LIFE!

However, the process is not quite complete . . .

There is no doubt about it, the past 90 days have been tough on
you. Your patience has been tested but your mind has remained
focused on the task at hand . . . namely, to put your financial
house in order, giving you the chance to live a confident financial
life without the fear of impending financial death.

THE NEW REALITY

As we fast approach a new millennium, a fanciful period of
new hopes and dreams, we are forced to consider and adjust to a
New Reality of two long-term trends that will undoubtedly affect
how your wages come in and go out of your wallet or purse: jobs
and healthcare.

Because corporate layoffs will continue to be, in good economic
times or bad, an inevitable fact of life, it will be tough for many
Americans to anticipate a bright financial future unless they have
prepared a solid financial plan . . . this reality check puts you way
ahead of the game.

Your *Wealth Workout* plan has considered the scenario of a job
loss and re-employment. You are prepared to adjust and financially survive, giving you the confidence to weather any downsizing storm. The importance of having enough money to financially
survive a healthcare emergency or long illness will continue to

grow in the minds of working Americans caught between the responsibilities of raising children and caring for aging parents . . . again, this reality for you remains in check because of the thoughtful consideration given to this area in your *Wealth Workout* plan.

In order to successfully complete the remainder of this workout it is important that we summarize three Wealth Building principles that will, if carried with you for the remainder of your life, guarantee a secure financial future:

DISCIPLINE — LONG-TERM THINKING — MAINTENANCE

DISCIPLINE

Any professional athlete will tell you that a successful exercise program requires a great deal of discipline, both in planning a routine and setting reasonable goals to perform it.

As you have learned through *Wealth Workout*, planning and goal setting are also required to prepare for a secure financial future.

To carry out a successful investment program, you must also adhere to the following disciplines.

Muster the Discipline to Pay Yourself First

Get out the tube of super glue and slap this one to the forehead because not only is it the most important of all considerations to a successful plan, but it is also the first to be forgotten. Be certain to *reward yourself first* by stashing away 20 percent of your monthly take-home pay *before* you pay the bills. In this manner, you will be certain to stay on the track of building your wealth portfolio.

Your bills can be paid with your remaining cash if you are willing to make cuts in your discretionary spending as we discussed in the Cut the Fat Workout (Weeks 4 and 5).

Twenty percent is too unrealistic for your budget? For some perhaps; but for the majority of wage earners, it is pure nonsense to cry and lament that you are not able to set aside some portion of your income for investment. Leave the whining for the politicians and GET BUSY CARVING OUT AT LEAST $25 A WEEK

($3.75 PER DAY) FOR YOUR FUTURE . . . a puny sum of cash that can easily grow, as demonstrated by Table 9–1.

TABLE 9-1: How Values Build When You Make Regular Investments of $100 a Month

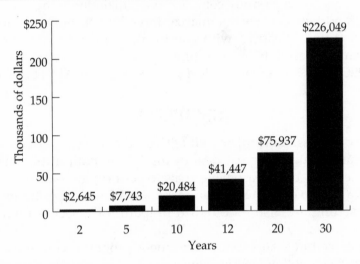

Assumes 10% annual rate of return, compounded monthly, with interest and dividends reinvested

Muster the Discipline to Live Within Your Means

The pressures of everyday life are great enough without imposing self-inflicted economic pressure on yourself to keep up with the Joneses. In other words, vow to live sensibly within your financial means. As former First Lady Nancy Reagan was fond of saying, "Just say No." In this case, just say no to excessive spending.

Today, living outside your means is too easily achieved as a result of credit cards. According to a report by John C. Norcross, a professor of psychology at the University of Scranton, "improving personal finances" was the number one New Year's resolution by Americans for 1994. The result? Americans charged a whopping *25 percent more* in 1994 than in 1993.

Pay down credit card debt as fast as possible! What may appear at the time of purchase to be "plastic power" will soon rear its ugly head as "plastic poison" because you have gone way over what your income can reasonably absorb. *If you don't have the cash, don't buy the trash.*

Muster the Discipline to Avoid Temptation

Most of us will remember the hallmark quip from comedian Flip Wilson, "The devil made me do it. "And so it goes today, as it was in the beginning: life titillates us time and time again with temptations designed to disrupt even the best-laid financial plans.

Whatever form your temptation takes, RESOLVE TO REMAIN A SAVER and do not revert back to being a spender.

Muster the Discipline to Recover from a Budget Buster

The reality remains that in spite of all efforts throughout the year to whittle down debt and keep discretionary spending in check, something will occur to bust your budget, such as your furnace breaking down two days before Christmas in balmy temperatures averaging 10 degrees Celsius.

The key to overcoming such a circumstance is to keep uppermost in your mind that you have prepared a financial plan for the long term, for all nine innings, for the whole enchilada.

Therefore, don't throw in the towel if you should experience such an unexpected loss. Pay for the expense from your emergency fund and replenish the fund as quickly as possible.

LONG-TERM THINKING

The degree of confidence you will have in your financial future will be directly related to how carefully you have constructed a long-term financial plan. And of course, the only way to maintain such a plan is to view it with a long-term frame of mind.

Long-term thinking applies to all investment age groups. Those on the younger side of the scale, fresh out of college, feisty with enthusiasm but short on discipline, will tend to rationalize their spending patterns with the belief that life is too short to worry about retirement. Unfortunately, life will unmercifully drag in old age if you are not financially prepared. After all, it takes cash to live, not merely survive.

On the other hand, time looks favorably upon the young rocket scientist who is willing to impose upon her- or himself a smidgen of discipline by putting together a modest investment portfolio.

Recall from the awesome power of *time and compounding* discussed in the Pump It Up Workout (Weeks 6 & 7) that the longer your cash is invested, the more it will produce. Table 9–2 is a startling example of the benefits of long-term thinking.

TABLE 9–2:   The Earlier You Start Investing for Retirement the More You Will Have

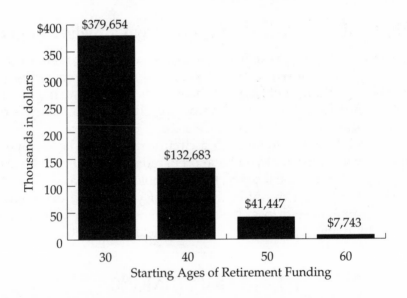

$100 per month invested earning 10%, compounded monthly, with interest and dividends reinvested. Assumes retirement at age 65.

Certainly, it is never too late to start investing. Even a modest nest egg is better than none at all. But the key point underscored by Table 9–2 is that THE EARLIER YOU START TO INVEST, THE LONGER AND HARDER YOUR MONEY CAN WORK FOR YOU.

Long-term thinking also requires your portfolio to remain aggressively invested in stock equities—quality common stocks of small, medium, and large corporations. If you recall from our previous discussion of equities, your approach to investing in securities for the long term is the only way for you to preserve the purchasing power of your money. Remember Figure 5–3 where we looked at six decades of performance of stocks, bonds, and bills compared to inflation?

Even a cursory review of the US stock market's history shows that like the tortoise in Aesop's fable, *the long-term investor wins in the end*.

A final thought of encouragement for you to keep in your long-term frame of mind is to *buy and hold*. Don't attempt to jump in and out of the market at the first whisper of bad news. Long-term investing's powerful ally, time, has proven to be a formidable steamroller for all the equity bumps the market will certainly encounter.

MAINTENANCE

The whole idea behind this final chapter is to offer some practical tips on the easiest way for you to PRESERVE AND SUPPORT THE CONTINUATION OF YOUR WEALTH WORKOUT ACHIEVEMENTS, not for the next 30 days, not for the next year, but for the remainder of your life! After all, what good is the pain if you are not able to enjoy the gain?

Ask any athlete his or her secret to bulging pecks or flat abs and the answer will be the same: maintenance. Ask any graduate of the University of Weight Loss how they manage to stay thin and trim: maintenance. Ask yourself how you plan to stay on your *Wealth Workout* track to success: maintenance.

Most of us find it bothersome and tedious to carry out a program after the enthusiasm and zip diminishes. We have made it easy for you to maintain your efforts and track your progress by providing you with a Seasonal Worksheet, an exercise that calls upon you to evaluate your progress during the Spring, Summer, and Fall. Winter is discussed later in the exercise. There is something magical about the change of seasons that serve as a reminder for you that life continues to roll along, that, "By golly, I *know* there's something I should be doing."

As certain as the seasons change, events in your life and the lives of family members will also change, which requires you to periodically review the impact of these changes on to the overall fitness of your *Wealth Workout* plan.

As an example, consider the following changes:

- **Your children.** Have you been blessed with your first? Does the oldest need braces? The broken window costs how much?

- **Your job.** Have you recently received a raise? Has your job been eliminated because of corporate downsizing? It costs *how* much to incorporate a business?

- **Medical concerns.** You stuck your finger in *what* machine? Your son has contracted an unidentifiable virus from *what* Third World country? A wage earner in the family has passed away?

- **Retirement.** Do you take the lump sum or the gold watch?

- **Home purchase.** Are you prepared to move up to larger digs as the kids grow? Have you saved the necessary amount of cash for closing? The inspector found *how* large of a crack in the foundation?

- **Inheritance.** Your distant uncle from Saudi Arabia bequeathed you the jewels to King *who*?

- **Taxes.** You were unable to document the majority of your itemized expenses and the IRS wants to audit you *when*?

We believe that as life rolls on, you will develop a seasonal habit of re-evaluating your financial health, an evaluation that considers your goals, the amount of money needed to achieve each goal, and a snapshot of funds accumulated to date.

────────────────────────┤ **Do This Now** ├────────────────

Examine the headings on your worksheet at the beginning of this exercise; they're very straightforward and simple to understand, wouldn't you say?

Before you begin to complete a seasonal section of your worksheet, make a master copy of the sheet for future checkups.

When either the first tulip opens, you chuck your first stone with the lawn mower, or the treetops begin to change color, stop your go-go life and conduct a seasonal evaluation.

You may be asking yourself, "OK, what happened to Winter?" The winter season not only offers you an opportunity to dream of sugarplums dancing in your head but also calls to mind the reality of tax collection and the arrival of 1040s and W-2s.

Winter is the period when you visit your personal trainer for an annual review. Give your trainer a call, set up an appointment, and begin to evaluate the progress you have made by working through the following questions:

- Are my goals still valid?
- Have I achieved any of my goals?
- Do I need to reprioritize?
- How is my cash flow holding up?
- How has my net worth changed?
- Do I need to recalculate how I plan to achieve any goal that has fizzled or needs a jump-start?
- Has additional expense fat crept into my daily budget?
- How are my investment options performing?
- Do I need to rethink my investment personality because I need a greater rate of return?
- What changes have occurred in the tax law that adversely affect my wealth? What are my options?
- Do I need to re-evaluate my insurance protection?

closing remarks

Now wasn't that fun? We *knew* you had what it took to complete the *Wealth Workout*!

As you have learned over the past 90 days, there really is no magic to the process of building a solid financial portfolio, or a solid body for that matter. You simply need to understand how your money or energy came in and where it went out.

Well, OK, there is admittedly a *little* more to the process than that, but when you boil down all of the instructions, tips, and cautions, the sensibility and strength of your long-term investment portfolio will continue to be based on a series of *choices*.

You have the ability to choose to

- Toss your *Wealth Workout* plan in a drawer with your old telephone books and forget about it or make the decision to maintain seasonal evaluations and annual reviews with your personal trainer.

- Ignore how you wastefully spend your discretionary cash or make the decision to examine the best way to build your emergency fund.

- Accept another credit card offering, a $5,000 line of credit, or make the decision to remain disciplined and debt free.

- Continue to believe that your government will be there for you at retirement or make the decision to claim your independence by building your own long-term nest egg.

The above choices, to include the ones that we have asked you to make throughout this workout, require you to MAKE A DECISION. Fortunately, *Wealth Workout* has provided you with the proper exercises to help you feel warm and comfortable with the decision-making process. If you should begin to feel the chills, discuss the decision with your personal trainer.

We are obviously mindful of the fact that it's your money. You have earned it. We only hope that you will carry with you the profitable information from *Wealth Workout* to help you be smart about how you spend it.

WEALTH WORKOUT
RECIPES

PORTFOLIOS VALUED UP TO $100,000

Bonds of Harmony

Asset Ingredients
57% US Bonds
20% US Stocks
13% International Stocks
10% Precious metals

Technique

Cut the first ingredient crosswise into several different mutual funds, combining with US stocks and favorite sauce in your portfolio. Stir well.

Cover and briefly refrigerate. Remove for heating.

Combine US stock and bond funds with a smatter of international spice over low heat for 10 years.

Serve with a sprinkle of precious metals.

Tangy Twist
Asset Ingredients
25% US Stocks
35% US Bonds
30% International Stocks
10% Precious metals

Technique
Combine the first three ingredients in your portfolio, mixing well.
Microwave at high, stirring in precious metals as needed.
Let stand, covered, for at least 15 years.

Lynn's Temptation
Asset Ingredients
40% US Stocks
10% US Bonds
40% International Stocks
10% Precious metals

Technique
Drop an aggressive growth stock fund into your boiling portfolio; return to a boil, adding an assortment of tangy international ingredients.

Reduce heat to medium-high for 20 years, adding a wedge of bonds.

Offer a side dish of precious metals.

PORTFOLIOS VALUED OVER $100,000

Old Fogy Cuisine
Asset Ingredients
60% US Bonds
17% US Stocks
16% International Stocks
3% Precious metals
2% Energy
2% Real estate

Technique

Combine the first three ingredients and bring to a fogy boil.

Cover, reducing heat to medium and simmer in portfolio for at least 10 years or until your international fund begins to flake.

Test occasionally by poking your investment advisor with a fork.

Gradually add some natural gas with perhaps a sprinkle of gold medallions.

Arrange for a slice of lakefront property for dessert.

Coddled Medley

Asset Ingredients
28% US Stocks
35% US Bonds
26% International Stocks
3% Energy
5% Precious metals
3 % Real estate

Technique

Sort and wash the first three ingredients, stirring together with a wire whisk.

Cook the stocks, bonds, and international funds at high heat for approximately 15 years.

Spoon in lightly tossed precious metals, while gradually adding an energy fund.

Top off with a slice of real estate.

Herbie's Delight

Asset Ingredients
38% US Stocks
10% US Bonds
36% International Stocks
5% Real estate
5% Energy
6% Precious metals

Technique

Heat a stock fund over medium-high heat, adding a pinch of precious metals.

Bring to a vigorous boil, stirring in a heaping portion of international spices and topping off with some bonds.

Cover, reducing heat to medium for approximately 20 years.

DO NOT OVERCOOK.

Sprinkle portfolio with a promising energy fund while gently adding select pieces of real estate.

APPENDIX

B

INVESTMENT OPTIONS

1. **Certificates of deposit** are FDIC insured and are sold by banks and will lock in a specific interest rate for a specified period of time. CDs are considered a temporary parking place for your money.

2. **Savings accounts** are FDIC insured and are offered by your local bank. The interest rates paid on these accounts are very low. According to the Bank Rate Monitor, passbook savings accounts pay a paltry average of 2.2 percent—way below the rate of inflation.

3. **Money market accounts** offer painfully low yields. These accounts have yielded to the ever-popular money market mutual fund (same flexibility, higher yields).

4. **Savings bonds** are guaranteed by the US government and are purchased from banks in amounts as low as $25. You earn a guaranteed rate of interest if you hold them five years. You don't owe federal taxes until you redeem the bond. You

may be able to avoid taxes entirely if you use the bond to pay for your child's education.

5. **US Treasury securities** (bills, notes, and bonds) are guaranteed by the US government, locking in a specific interest rate with a promise to return your principal at maturity. Other than in Tennessee, earned interest is excluded from state income tax.

   Bills have maturities of less than one year, do not pay interest, and are discounted from their face value at the time of purchase. You are paid the full face value at maturity. The difference between the purchase price and face value is your yield.

   Notes have maturities of 2–10 years. You receive an interest check every six months until maturity, at which time you are paid your principal.

   Bonds have maturities of 10–30 years. You receive an interest check every six months until maturity, when you receive the face value of the bond.

6. **Mortgage-backed securities** are instruments with popular names such as Ginnie Mae Freddie Mac, representing pools of mortgages backed by the government.

7. **Municipal bonds** are issued by a city, county, or state government to finance public works projects on behalf of the municipality. The interest from these bonds is not taxed by the federal government.

8. **Zero coupon bonds** are sold at deep discount by corporations and governments. The value increases until it matures. You receive no interest but must pay taxes on the interest as it builds every year, commonly known as phantom income.

9. **Corporate bonds** are issued by American corporations. Most pay higher interest than government bonds. The longer the term of the bond, the higher your interest rate. Corporate bonds with high ratings (AA or AAA), as rated by Standard & Poor or Moody. Bonds with lower ratings are better known as *junk bonds*.

10. **US large cap equities**, those equities with market capital in the billions, are generally the well-established companies that pay dividends, which are considered income. As part of the "Standard & Poor's 500 index," these blue-chip stock companies are not as aggressive as are small and midcaps, but you still need to accept the natural market cycles and day-to-day price fluctuations of a stock investment.

11. **Real estate** can be purchased for investment purposes through REITs (real estate investment trusts) or real estate limited partnerships.

12. **International bonds and stocks** are securities issued by foreign countries in foreign currencies.

13. **US mid cap equities** those equities with market capital exceeding $1 billion, have recently raised the interest of novice and professional investors alike. Largely ignored because of their wedge between the sexy small caps and the hefty (large caps), the mid cap includes companies that have captured their own profitable market niche.

    As of 1991, they have also earned their own index, the "Mid cap 400 index." According to a new study by Wilshire Associates, a Los Angeles stock-research firm, mid cap stocks have outperformed both small- and large cap stocks since 1985. Should this trend continue, mid cap performance would dilute the widely held notion that small cap stocks always bring the highest rate of return over time.

14. **Junk bonds** are corporate bonds with low or no ratings by Standard and Poor or Moody. Any bond rated below Baa by Moody or below BBB by Standard and Poor is considered a junk bond.

15. **US small cap equities**, those equities with market capital of $100–$350 million, have provided the highest historical average annual returns. These companies, typically found in the "Russell 2000 index," represent a more aggressive investment, and, as you might expect, the rates of return have paid off handsomely in the past.

16. **Futures and option contracts** gamble on what something will cost in the future and are sold in the commodities

markets. Professional money managers and sophisticated investors use these strategies. They are not recommended for inexperienced investors.

17. **Precious metals and energy** offer investors an inflation hedge and can be purchased through limited partnerships or by purchasing stocks or mutual funds of mining and energy companies.

MUTUAL FUNDS BY FUND OBJECTIVE

1. **Money market funds** invest in securities that mature in less than one year: Treasury bills, CDs, commercial paper. They are safer than any other mutual fund. Money market funds are the best place to park your money for short-term financial goals of less than three years.

2. **Government bond funds** invest in US government obligations including T-bills, T-notes, T-bonds, GNMAs, and FNMAs. The average maturity of a security in a bond fund will differ significantly based on the fund objective. You should match your time horizon to an appropriate fund with the appropriate securities.

3. **Municipal bond funds** invest in notes and bonds issued by municipalities. The interest earned from these funds is generally tax exempt from federal income tax. There are different types of municipal bond funds with different average maturities. These funds are used by individuals in high tax brackets. To compare a municipal bond fund to a

government or corporate bond fund, you must compare tax equivalent yields.

4. **Corporate bond funds** invest in bonds issued by corporations. The amount of gain or loss of high-quality corporate bond funds depends upon the average maturity of the bonds in the fund. Risk increases as average maturity increases due to interest rate fluctuations. Corporate bond funds have a higher degree of risk than government bond funds and therefore offer a higher yield.

5. **High-yield corporate bond funds** invest in bonds issued by corporations with low or no ratings by Standard & Poor or Moody (all called junk bonds). Any bond rated "Baa" or higher by Moody's or "BBB" or higher by Standard & Poor is considered investment quality; all others are considered junk bonds. The higher the bond rating, the lower the interest rate it pays.

6. **International bond funds** invest in bonds issued by foreign countries in foreign currency. Since foreign markets do not necessarily move in tandem with US markets, each country represents varying investment opportunities at different times.

7. **Global bond funds** invest in bonds issued all over the world, including the United States. These funds seek higher interest rates in countries with currency strength against the US dollar and are politically and economically stable.

8. **Growth funds** invest in US common stocks and seek capital appreciation. Growth-investing funds look for stocks that show high levels of profit growth, stocks that are undervalued based on the companies earnings or book value.

9. **Growth and income funds** invest in well-established US companies that pay relatively high cash dividends to produce both capital appreciation and current income.

10. **Equity income funds** invest in US stocks that focus on current income.

11. **International equity funds** invest in stocks of foreign companies, while global equity funds invest in both foreign

and US stocks. Some are broadly diversified among many countries, while some specialize in a particular region or country.

12. **Aggressive growth funds** invest in emerging growth companies in the United States that are striving for maximum capital growth using aggressive trading strategies.

13. **Small company funds** invest primarily in stocks of small companies. These funds and aggressive growth funds often outperform other categories of US stocks during a bull market but suffer greater losses during bear markets.

14. **Sector funds** invest in US stocks of a specific industry including financial, health, natural resources, metals, technology and utilities, or stocks of a specific country.

15. **Index funds** purchase stock in companies included in a specific market average or "index" such as the S&P 500, mirroring the movement of the market.

16. **Balanced (total return) funds** invest in US common stocks and bonds and offer neither the worst nor the best of individual bond and stock funds.

17. **Asset allocation funds** invest in a strategic allocation of different stocks and bonds in an effort to reduce risk and stabilize returns.

18. **Equity REITs** are real estate investment trust funds that own income-producing real estate. Some specialize in particular types of property. REITs pay dividends, are considered a form of mutual fund, and offer investors an inflation hedge.

19. **UITs** purchase bonds that are held for the life of the trust, offering a stable income stream.

LIST OF TABLES
AND FIGURES

Index